UNIFIED
IN HOPE

UNIFIED IN HOPE

arabs and jews talk about peace

interviews by
CAROL J. BIRKLAND
foreword by Ghassan Rubeiz

FRIENDSHIP PRESS ● NEW YORK

Library of Congress Cataloging-in-Publication Data

Unified in hope.

1. Israel—Arab conflicts. I. Birkland, Carol J.,
1945–
DS119.7.U49 1987   956'.04   87-19680
ISBN 0-377-00177-5

North American Edition by Friendship Press
Editorial Office: 475 Riverside Drive (772)
                   New York, NY 10115

Distribution Office: PO Box 37844
                     Cincinnati, OH 45222-0844

Cover design: Rob Lucas

ISBN 0-377-00177-5

© 1987 WCC Publications, World Council of Churches.
150 route de Ferney, 1211 Geneva 20, Switzerland

Printed in the United States of America

Contents

Foreword

Most of the literature on the Arab/Jewish conflict is written to win support for one side or the other. In recent years, however, some writing has addressed the two sides as parallel legitimate causes. This recent "moderate" literature is in sharp contrast to the normal lot, which I would call the literature of "scoring". Scoring literature attempts to achieve maximum credit points for one side and maximum debit points for the other side.

Jewish "scoring" literature tends to emphasize points like these:
— The continuous presence of Jews in Israel for over four thousand years.
— The persecution of the Jews of the diaspora, and the Holocaust as the climax of this persecution.
— The fulfilment of God's promise in the return of the "Land" to the "Chosen" people.
— The phenomenal contribution of the Jews to the development of the land and to the welfare of the world. "They deserve a land of their own."
— Arab "failure" to make peace with the Jews when they were willing to negotiate for peace.
— The importance of the present and future security of Israel for the Jewish and Western worlds.

Scorers for the Arab side have no difficulty in developing parallel arguments:
— For two thousand years, since Roman times, Palestinians have been a majority in "historic Palestine", which is now "Israel".
— The establishment of Israel has been at the expense of the Palestinians. There are today two million Palestinians in the diaspora, 1.2 million in the territories under Israeli occupation, and 700,000 Pales-

tinian Israelis under Israeli rule. The Jews have displaced Palestinians through wars and other coercive means.
— Palestinians are now ready to compromise and accept a share of the land (about 20 per cent) in the West Bank, Gaza and East Jerusalem. Israel "refuses" to negotiate for peace.
— Palestinians belong to Palestine. They do not wish to be sent away to other Arab countries.
— Palestinian nationhood is as valid as Zionist nationhood, if not more, when viewed in terms of a common history, language, culture, etc.
— In Israel and the occupied "territories" there are two million Palestinians (Arabs). How can Israel absorb them? They are not equal citizens nor are they free to choose their own system of government. Underlying the different views about the political situation is the belief that the people on the other side are "bad people", "repulsive people". And those on our own side all "good people".

The moderate literature recognizes the legitimacy of both nationhoods, the needs of both communities for freedom and security, the possibility to share the land, and the pragmatism of peace which is based on justice. Writers who see both sides of the arguments show how history has been viewed differently by both communities. Jews, for example, stress the earlier stages of history, and the Palestinians the more recent. Similarly, these writers point to the many ways in which religion can be used to justify claims of ownership of land. For example, the Bible is a record of Jewish continuity in the Holy Land, but it is also about love and justice for all.

As time passes, the conflict deepens through more wars, more displaced people and more confrontation. The advocates of force become stronger and they urge both sides to "fight until victory".

The literature of "scoring points" appears more persuasive than the literature of moderation. It is in continuity with the experience of the people. People on either side are brought up to believe that only their side of the story is correct. Parents, religious leaders and the mass media reinforce the stereotypes. Extreme views are easier to understand. They are seen to reflect one's own preferences and anxieties. There are few day-to-day human contacts between the Arabs and the Jews. The battle front and the court rooms are the usual meeting places. The newspapers and television purvey prejudices and deal in hate. And people hate by hearsay.

Since the Israeli war of 1982 in Lebanon there has been a change in attitude. The experience of Israeli soldiers in Lebanon has convinced at least a segment of the population in the country of the cruelty of war, the helplessness of refugees and the complexity of the social factors which perpetuate conflict. The new war angered some soldiers; quite a number saw the absurdity of occupying new land. Still others had the chance to see first-hand something of the sufferings of people, especially women and children in vulnerable conditions. The demonstration by some 400,000 people in Tel Aviv against the war was a milestone in Arab/Israeli relations.

During the last few years, there has been a growing sympathy towards each other. When an Arab speaks about a positive experience with a Jew and when a Jew talks about a pleasant encounter with an Arab, the mask of prejudice drops and they discover each other's humanity and the face of God in both communities. It is a slow process of rediscovering each other's humanity, and it is a sign of hope.

Peace movements in the West have been too busy with the issue of the "final war" to give adequate attention to the ongoing wars of the Middle East. The conventional wars of the Middle East may well lead to nuclear confrontation, if current trends are not halted. But that is by no means the only reason why people in the West should take a greater interest in developments there. They have a moral responsibility.

Moderate literature is good material for peace education. And peace education is an urgent need. That is why books like this one are important. Here, for example, are portraits of people who are not afraid to share with others their hopes and their dreams. They talk about their families and childhood experiences; they tell us about their work and their concerns. They are not afraid to cross borders and to make points of contact.

The book comes out of an ecumenical initiative. Both the process of gathering material and the presentation of the material are guided by the following objectives:

— To expose a diversity of views on the Arab/Israeli situation by articulate leaders, who have demonstrated concrete interest in peace.

— To demonstrate that fear is the deepest factor in the motivation of people on both sides of the issue. Such a recognition has crucial implications in dealing with the political problem.

— To show that despite the conflict and difference of opinion, the views expressed are legitimate, rational and worthy to be heard.

— To capture prophetic insights, which might generate dialogue, and lead to attitude changes.

— To identify basic differences between the moderate representatives of the two communities and to present them frankly.

— To generate in the reader a feeling of compassion for both sides.

— To inform and inspire potential recruits to peace education and reconciliation in the Middle East conflict.

— To allow for Palestinians and Israelis to reach towards each other through the vicarious medium of this book. The Palestinians and the Jews are each other's best healers, just as much as they are each other's worst enemies. They must look into each other's eyes.

Implicit in this book is the thesis that there is no solution to the Palestinian/Israeli problem without a social or spiritual breakthrough, which alone will change people's views about one another.

We are deeply indebted to Carol Birkland for a delicate task sensitively undertaken and a difficult job well done.

GHASSAN RUBEIZ

Introduction

Of all the political conflicts that occupy the world's attention today, none seems more intractable than that between Palestinian Arabs and Israeli Jews.

Beginning in 1920 with Arab riots in Jerusalem, the ensuing years have been a period characterized by an uninterrupted pattern of conflict and violence. It is not necessary to provide a chronology here, but only to say that rarely has the world witnessed a regional conflict so resistant to resolution yet so universally threatening.

Having spent a good deal of time in the area, I found myself lately becoming less and less hopeful about the possibility of peace for the Israelis and Palestinians. Specifically, where before I had eagerly read all of the news reports and political analyses, I now lacked the emotional energy to absorb any more stories of stalled peace processes or the latest in the all-too-familiar pattern of violence avenged by more violence.

I was not alone; other people I knew felt the same way. As much as we cared about both Israelis and Palestinians, we were on the verge of simply not being able to take any more of this conflict. All of us had heard too much political rhetoric — from both sides. We had heard too many "selective" historical accounts, too much negative stereotyping, and more than enough self-righteous blaming.

Listening to both sides recite their interpretations of the conflict's history, it becomes readily apparent how, from the beginning, each side chose to deal with the other, not as individuals with specific historical experiences, but as narrowly defined communities. For Arabs, Jews were foreign interlopers and agents of European imperial powers. For Jews, Arabs were dishonest, lazy and primitive — but in a charming sort of way.

As the conflict continued and intensified, attitudes solidified to the point that today each side dismisses the other as terrorist, racist, or worse. Stereotypes are not challenged because, in the most basic sense, both sides need them. Most Israelis and Palestinians have no desire to relate to each other on anything other than collective terms. To do so would risk the possibility of upsetting thought patterns that provide security in a less than secure environment.

In their heart of hearts, many Israelis and Palestinians dream of the day when the other side will simply go away, thus solving all problems. Today that fantasy is more actually threatening to the Palestinian population who see in the Israeli parliament elected representatives advocating their expulsion to Jordan and elsewhere.

On the other hand, the Palestinian fantasy of a homeland free of Jews, while less of a possibility considering Israeli military strength, has inhibited the kind of realistic thinking that could have served as a basis for a unified political agenda.

Recently, for example, a young Palestinian student from a West Bank university expressed the opinion that when the secular-democratic Palestinian state is established in what is now Israel, the West Bank, and Gaza, all of the Jews who were in that area prior to 1917 would be allowed to stay. All the others, which of course means the bulk of the current Jewish population, would have to leave.

Finally, both sides have been deceived by violence. The Palestinians resort to it because, viewing themselves as powerless, violence makes them feel, if only fleetingly, powerful. Israelis use violence because it makes them feel secure. But violence has not procured the power or the security both sides desire. Instead, it has condemned all to a seemingly endless cycle of cruelty and revenge.

There are, however, some Israelis and Palestinians who confound all of the old stereotypes by rejecting the urge towards violence and hate. They exhort Israelis and Palestinians alike to adopt new ways of relating to each other before it is too late. Above all, they are convinced that peace is possible.

At this juncture in the conflict, I personally felt a need to make contact with these peace-makers — not only to listen to what they had to say, but to try to undertand how they had managed to escape the hate and fear that imprison so many others. What had happened in their lives that gave them the rare ability to understand and empathize with their enemies?

Then I thought about all of the other people who shared my discouragement about the possibility for peace, and that is why I decided it was important to let the peace-makers, few as they may be, speak. Perhaps what was needed now was not yet another political and social commentary about the conflict, but a book about people — not written about them but in their own words.

This was the skeletal idea I brought to Dr Ghassan Rubeiz at the Middle East desk of the World Council of Churches when I was studying at the Bossey Ecumenical Institute. He enthusiastically supported the plan, added some ideas of his own, and the project was begun.

Together we made a list of people I was to interview. Many on the list we knew personally, some we knew only from their writings or through other friends. A list of general questions was prepared. But instead of asking for political opinions, we were interested in getting to know these people personally. What was their family history? What had their parents told them about Israelis/Palestinians, and were those views confirmed when they finally met and got to know Arabs or Jews? If it were somehow possible to explain one thing about themselves and their community that would be guaranteed to be understood by the opposing side, what would it be? What were their dreams, and what were their fears?

Travelling last summer to Israel, the occupied West Bank, and Gaza, I contacted the people on our list and solicited their involvement in the project. I was amazed at each person's willingness, not only to cooperate (in fact, they were all extremely enthusiastic about the possibility), but to entrust their personal feelings and stories to me. I have tried mightily to justify that trust.

Because of their willingness to share of themselves, the reader is about to meet a group of truly remarkable people. Reading their stories, one marvels at their ability to remain human in a situation where each day humaneness is threatened. Unlike the majority of the area's inhabitants, they view this conflict, not as prisoners of history, but as people who are able to put history in perspective, realizing that if one only continues to dwell on the certainties of the past, possibilities for the future will be lost.

Speaking the truths that most refuse to hear, one is soon struck by the prophetic dimension of their thoughts. Above all, they destroy stereotypes and challenge attitudes that for so long have resisted change.

Are they prophets? I don't know. If one of the classical definitions of prophets is that they are not accepted by their own people, then perhaps the description is apt. The great tragedy is that their views are, by and large, not accepted or supported by their own respective communities.

One thing, however, is abundantly clear. If we say that blessings are gifts bestowed upon us by God, then without a doubt these people are

God's gifts because, having encountered them, I left feeling as though I had indeed been blessed. My hope is that the reader will be able to share that blessing.

Ultimately these people are blessings because they bring hope. My final question to each of them was: "Are you hopeful that peace will come?" In one way or another they all replied affirmatively. Many responded with another question: "What choice is there other than hope?" they asked.

Their hope is not naive hope; it is not the kind of hope which bases itself on eventual results. Rather it is a radical — some might even say irrational — hope that refuses to die even though there are times when it sees only hopelessness.

From a particularly Christian view, St Paul knew about this kind of hope. In the eighth chapter of his letter to the Romans he wrote: "For in this hope we were saved. Now hope that is seen is not hope. For who hopes for what he sees? But if we hope for what we do not see, we wait for it with patience."

St Paul, Minnesota USA   CAROL J. BIRKLAND

Acknowledgments

There are many persons whose help made this book possible. First of all thanks must go to the Bush Foundation of St Paul, Minnesota, who awarded me a fellowship without which I could never have attempted such a project.

Secondly, I must thank my colleagues in the Division for World Mission and Inter-Church Cooperation of The American Lutheran Church in Minneapolis, Minnesota, who encouraged me and cheerfully accepted extra work so I could take time off to study at the Bossey Ecumenical Institute and complete this book.

I am grateful to Dr Ghassan Rubeiz of the World Council of Churches in Geneva who, from the beginning, shared my enthusiasm for this project and helped guide it on to the printed page.

My husband Tom and my friend Ann Hafften encouraged me when I needed it most: after a book containing invaluable notes, names, addresses, phone numbers, and interview dates was left behind in a Jerusalem taxi and never seen again. Ann helped with editing and they both read and critiqued the manuscript.

Finally, my thanks go to the members of Kibbutz Kfar Menachem of the Kibbutz Ha'artzi movement who for the past ten years have welcomed me as one of their own. It was through their experiences that I first began to understand the tragedy and complexity of the Israeli/Palestinian conflict. Never once in all that time did they either dehumanize or delegitimize the Palestinian community, so that when the time came I met Palestinians with an open mind, free of the destructive, negative stereotypes that have corrupted the thoughts of so many.

Mary Khass

Mary Khass, 59, is a Haifa-born Palestinian. She works for the United Nations Relief and Works Agency (UNRWA) in Gaza where she administers kindergarten programmes for Palestinian refugee children. One of her programmes, called MUMS (Mothers Understanding Methods of Schooling), helps mothers teach conceptional learning to their children.

In 1984 Khass participated in the United Nations' conference marking the end of the Women's Decade in Nairobi, Kenya. There, she appeared along with an Israeli woman at a forum to discuss the Israeli/Palestinian conflict.

In her encounters with Jews, Khass tries to understand their fears. "I always try to understand what bothers them. Why are they uneasy and refusing the two-state solution?" she asks. "I also wonder why it is so difficult for us Palestinians to understand why they are going through these fears?"

When I was young, I remember one of my Jewish friends said: "You know, you don't look like an Arab." I asked her if she didn't think that was a racist remark. She was so embarrassed. She said: "That's not what I meant. I meant the way you act, the way you behave."

I said: "What do I act like? I act like a human person, an individual. I have individuality — you do too. It has nothing to do with my being Palestinian or Jewish or German or whatever. And I want to remind you that the most valid community and people on earth are the Jews because you are a combination of so many nations that are trying to learn how to live together."

* * *

Number one, I am proud of who I am. Never for one minute did I want to be any other person than a Palestinian woman. There are people who are sometimes so afraid or ashamed or humiliated that at a certain point they may deny who they are. I am not afraid, and I am proud because I am a Palestinian.

Some Israelis have said to me: "But you see, you are different from the other Arabs." And I say: "No, I represent the majority of the Palestinians. Believe me, I do."

"Why don't we know more people like you?" they ask. And I say: "Because you don't want to know."

* * *

When I retire, I have decided that I want to write a book about my experiences. A lot of history would be there, and it would be a very human history because it would tell of encounters between people — especially my encounters with Jewish people. What really bothers them? Why do they refuse the two-state solution? What are their fears? Why is it so difficult for us Palestinians to understand why they are going through those fears? These are the things you learn when you talk to each other.

This land here has been ours for generations. When you give part of your land and willingly say: "Okay, I compromise, and I'm willing to give up part of this land", then, as the person who is compromising, it's not easy to understand that the other person still has fears.

When you talk about the two-state solution, somebody — a Jewish person — will say, "Well, why didn't you accept it in 1948? Why did you do this in 1948? What happened when you did this and this and this?" So I try to explain it to them, and these answers are really very historical and very important for many people who do not know the real conflict. It is important to see the conflict through these face-to-face encounters.

That is what made our dialogue in Nairobi so successful. It was because I was able to talk to the Jewish person in the diaspora. There were so many of these women — so many from all over the world and all of them Jewish. They came wanting to know what was going on. "Who is this Palestinian woman who is going to convince us?" they asked. And it was really wonderful. I learned a lot from their questions; you have no idea how educational it was for me.

* * *

I was born in Haifa and my father was one of the very first men who went to school and university at that time. He went to the American University; then it was not in Beirut but in Sidon. He went on horseback and camel. He became the headmaster of a school in Haifa, and that is how I lived in Haifa most of my life. I come from a Christian family, but I am married to a Muslim.

My family originally was Protestant and because of that we were a minority, but unfortunately during the Mandate we were a very elite minority. During the Mandate, the British spoiled the Protestant Church so I was brought up to feel superior. I did not stay that way for long.

I was quite young when I revolted, so to speak, against the church's traditional "do's and don'ts". I must admit, I was quite a big problem for my father. I am his eldest child and I refused to accept those very discriminating traditions. As Protestants we were supposed to be against Roman Catholics and against Orthodox, against Muslims — against a certain class of people and so on and so forth. And that was the argument I had with my father. "This kind of thinking", I said, "is all so much against what you are teaching me as a good Christian, so I won't agree with you unless you show me that you really believe in all of this by doing it."

My father was an educated person and he wanted to give me education, but he also wanted to give me all of his experience. The world was progressing and he was imposing all these limitations about what he thought was good and not good for me. I was revolting against the social structure of the Palestinian middle class family. I have always wanted to do things that people did not dare do; I have to admit that. For instance, I was the first Palestinian woman who wore trousers in Haifa.

* * *

It is so personal but I do not mind sharing it. Traditionally, in our culture, if a young man sees a woman and he likes her and he thinks her family has the same status as his, he will just come and ask for her hand. That is what happened when I was 16. I was still studying then.

I remember that my father came to talk to me, to convince me to say yes to a young man who I thought was very limited and very stupid. I kept asking my father: "But why? Why him? He doesn't relate to anything that you believe in."

His answer turned my world upside down. He said: "He comes from a good family and they are owners of property " And I said: "Well, I don't

want him. I don't like him. I can't stand him and I won't marry him."
My father thought I was too young to decide for myself — that is what
he told me later. But the method he used with me was: "But I said, 'Yes,
you would marry him'."
So what I did was run away to my uncle. I said that I didn't want to
marry, I wanted to study. My uncle protected me and he told my father:
"If you keep doing this to her, she will run away — then what?"
That changed a lot in my life. First, I vowed to myself that I would
decide — no matter what pressure — who I was going to marry, and
second, I would never marry before I was 25 years old.
The pressure from the family was incredible. Almost every week there
was somebody else for me to marry and all for various reasons: sometimes wealth, sometimes relations, sometimes status or whatever. But
every time I refused and I am not sorry. I think this is what changed my
way of seeing life.
The reason I became a feminist is mainly because of that experience. I
felt: "Why shouldn't I decide who I want to marry when my brother who
is younger can decide?" This whole experience brought me closer to
understanding the world of women, and I began to think about equality,
and women's freedom.

* * *

When I grew up, we lived in an area where we had Jewish neighbours.
Since they were Orthodox, they would call me to go and put off and put
on the light for the Sabbath. And there were times, let me be honest —
most of those times, I was a child and in the middle of playing — when I
pretended I did not hear them. But my mother was there and she would
say: "That's not nice. That is not neighbourly and that's not Christian.
You have to be good to your neighbours."
I remember also that my very first contacts with Jews came when they
began arriving from Europe. My father once told us that he saw a doctor
sweeping the floors and I asked why. He explained that because this
man's certificate to practise was from Germany, he could not work here.
He was Jewish and my father told me about the discrimination against
the Jews in Germany. This made me remember back to the days when
we had had Armenians coming to our door begging for food and shelter.
So I understood that what was happening to the Jews was something like
what the Armenians had been through — the massacre in Turkey and so
on.

That was the time I began to sympathize with people who had lost their human rights. I began to understand the value of human rights so that, even when I was very young, I took time to read most of the United Nations material on human rights. Much of it I don't think I understood. But what was important for me was that it opened my eyes and what I read related to Christianity. You know, the very first song we learned in Sunday school was "Jesus loves the little children, all the children of the world."

I must tell you the truth. I am not religious — not any more. But I must say I owe a lot to my Christian upbringing. At least it taught me about equality and human rights. I think my revolt was not against Christianity and its teachings. My revolt was against what Christianity or any other religion has become. What we people have made of it.

* * *

It was very shocking to me when in 1948, immediately after the establishment of the state of Israel, I was walking in the German colony in Haifa and there was a siren for an air raid. I did not want to hide in the shelter and just kept going because my house was very near.

I was arrested by the Israeli guards and taken to the headquarters. We got into a very hot argument. The Jewish woman soldier there was very articulate, but very vicious. I remember her very well. We were arguing about what was happening to the Palestinians — their land being taken and their being forced out. And I said: "But you know, you have been through the Holocaust. How can you treat people like this?"

She turned to me — it's so vivid — she was climbing up the stairs and she turned half way round and said: "Maybe it's because of that."

Her expression and the way she said it made me think. It took me some time to realize that because of what had happened to them, some of the Jews were taking revenge on us.

I kept feeling sorry for myself for quite a while after the establishment of the Israeli state. I was angry at myself for ever having sympathy for the Jewish people during the pre-state period. It took me some time to grow out of that and realize that they were behaving like that to protect themselves and they are still doing that now.

* * *

Two things are happening now in the Israeli community. First, people are becoming more and more reactionary in their attitudes, but beside that you see the people who really have a conscience. That only means that the struggle inside Israel is going to take much longer than we really want simply because they have to go through the process of first feeling victorious, then feeling superior, basking in their sense of achievement: "We have a state, it is beautiful, it is ours, we can do with it what we want." Later on there will come that time when they will say: "OK, what about others?"

Unfortunately, the majority of Israelis are against that very small humanitarian voice. Why? Because the Zionist state, in order to protect itself, has been re-educating the Jewish people.

The state of Israel points at us as the enemies and tells the Israelis: "If you do not keep up militarization, your state will not exist any more."

That kind of education, I think, has really made all of the Jewish people very nervous. Sometimes, when I am speaking to Israelis, they say: "What guarantees will you give us to prove that you will not fight us again, after you have your state beside our state?"

And I laugh because it is really funny. They are the number three military power in the world and they ask me that question! Many of them really do believe it. It used to make me feel really disgusted. "How can you say that when you are the oppressor," I'd think, "when you are beating me and have been beating me since 1948. How can you still ask me that?"

* * *

I worked through all of my anger and was able to understand how the Jews felt by knowing and living with them, and also by being open with them about all the issues that divide us. I have read a lot about the Holocaust, and that gave me a very good idea of how and why the Jewish people feel the way they do. Menachem Begin made the Holocaust into a very political tool and he used it to play on Israeli fears. Because of those fears, a lot of Israelis have become arrogant, superior and selfish. But all of this is against their own social and community structure. It is so clear if you see what is happening in Israel. They have been training this generation and the generation before to solve their problems in the only way they know: by power. In the army they use the same methods against the Palestinians, and now they are using these methods against themselves.

The Jews in the diaspora are in a unique situation because for them the state of Israel is the dream. It is what they have dreamed of all of their lives, and physically and emotionally they refuse to admit that Israel has become a powerful and attacking state. I don't want to call it a racist state — but I will say it is a discriminating state. And the Jews in the diaspora don't want to accept this fact. They refuse it. You must understand that the Jews are really afraid. They feel that if they close both eyes, if they don't keep one eye open, the state of Israel is not going to be there.

They need to learn that the only way to protect their state is by peace — peace with the Arab world but peace, mainly and most of all, with the Palestinians. That is what they have to realize. I tell them: "You have tried war for the last forty years. You have slept literally with the gun under your pillow. So what?"

What the Israelis are doing now is, because of their relation with the United States, erasing the independent element in their state. What they don't realize — I think their leaders do, but the Israelis themselves also need to realize it — is that America is not pro-Israel. America is Israel's worst enemy. America is giving them money and arms not because they support Israel, but because it is much cheaper for the United States to have Israel do its dirty work. Through that process, Israel is losing its independence and its identity.

* * *

Yes, I think the Israelis who I know really understand me. At least there is trust. For instance, when anything happens in the refugee camps here, I get at least ten calls from various Israeli groups asking if there is a way they can help. If there is a curfew in one of the camps, I say: "Yes, you are an Israeli woman. Come. Bring milk, bring water, bring vegetables. There is one hour of break at mid-day. I can't go and throw food across the barbed wire but you can as Jews." And they do it.

There are a lot of people who want to help, who are moderate and progressive on human rights. You see lots of these groups. But I keep explaining to them in one way or another, mildly, bit by bit, that they are on a guilt trip. What they would like to do is protect the achievements, the victories of Israel. They want the state to stay as it is, but they want to be humane as well, and it just cannot be. As long as they don't recognize our rights as human beings, and as long as they are arrogant, and as long as inside they feel and believe that they are superior, they will never be able to live in peace here.

Unless they realize that we have made all the compromises that could be made by us as people, they will never accept the Palestinian state.

What is more important, and I'm really very open with them about this, is that they have been through one Holocaust. They have to recognize that we are going through much the same. Definitely we have not had so many millions of people killed, but we are suffering terribly, and there is no law in the world that says we should not fight occupation. It is every human being's right to fight occupation, just like the Israelis fought the British. Now it is our time to fight occupation, and the Israelis must know that, in the end, the Palestinians cannot be beaten.

* * *

It is not as if we Palestinians don't have problems — we do. For instance, when we heard the news that Jews had demonstrated against the Sabra and Shatilla massacre, some Palestinians said: "Oh, they don't mean it."

Why was it so difficult for us to accept and believe? It is difficult because we are oppressed, and when you are oppressed you distrust. You can imagine there is a lot of distrust; Palestinians can't believe that there are Jews who do such things.

Now it is getting a little better. I remember an argument I had with some Palestinians and I said: "Listen, during Sabra and Shatilla, when our women demonstrated in Jordan they were shot at. In no place in the Arab world were our people allowed to demonstrate. Here, the Jews demonstrated against Sabra and Shatilla and against their own government. That should tell us something; that should teach us some lessons."

* * *

What would I tell the Israelis? I would tell them that since we both love this land, let's learn how to live together. Let's learn how to make both our states good enough, democratic enough, beautiful enough for us to share the land rather than destroy it. I would also tell them that they, their parents, and their grand-parents have gone through what we are going through now.

Let me tell you why the Israelis do not have to fear me. I want identity and I want roots. I want to develop as a nation, and I don't want to go to wars. As long as I have what I want, my rights — my human rights, my national rights — why do I have to go to wars?

We are not big nations — either of us. We are not the Soviet Union and the United States. We don't have interests anywhere in the world except on this one beautiful spot. As long as they recognize my rights as a human being, why should I want to fight the Israelis?

Israel should be the only nation that recognizes what it means to be rootless. They should be the only people who recognize what it means to be without an identity. And they should really know what it means to be discriminated against, harassed and oppressed. That is why they should trust me.

Mordechai Bar-On

*After a distinguished 22-year military career and ten years as an executive in the Jewish Agency, Col. **Mordechai Bar-On** was elected to the Knesset in 1984. During the past few years, he has become one of the leading spokespersons for the Peace Now movement and serves on the executive of the International Centre for Peace in the Middle East, in Tel Aviv.*

"What I have to do", says Bar-On, "is influence and try to change Israeli attitudes. I also have to convey to the PLO leadership my honest feeling that they too have to change if they want to achieve even their minimum goals. If they understand that, I am a real partner for them because that is my goal too."

Bar-On, 58, was born in Israel and has an MA in international affairs from Columbia University. While working on his doctorate, he lectured (1983-84) at the Hebrew University on Israeli foreign and security policy. Bar-On has recently resigned his Knesset seat to pursue more fully his teaching and writing career.

Between 1948 and 1967 there was no real chance for peace. Because Israel would not pay the price that might make it interesting for the Arabs, and the Arabs would not give up the hope that they might be able to start another war and defeat Israel.

The results of the 1967 war changed all that. For the first time we had something to give back. Unfortunately, nobody accepted what we wanted to give, but after 1967 work for peace began to have a more active meaning.

In 1962 or 1963 there was a woman who organized dialogues with Palestinians in her home in Tel Aviv. A number of Jewish peaceniks and Palestinian Arabs would sit down and talk, and I always went there wearing my army uniform. I remember one of the Arabs who came was quite a well-known Bedouin sheikh, and he couldn't get over the fact that I attended and would go to the military governor in Be'er Sheva telling him that he met Col. Bar-On at these meetings.

I went to the meetings because they were not public. If they had been public, the army regulation would have prohibited me from attending, but since the meetings were held in a private home, there was no problem.

Over the years I became more acquainted with Arabs. After 1967, there were more opportunities, and by then I could count quite a number of Arab people I meet quite regularly, both in the West Bank and from the Israeli Arab community.

Three years ago I met Abu Iyad in Budapest when a delegation from the International Centre for Peace in the Middle East visited there as guests of the Hungarian peace movement. Abu Iyad has been heavily involved in terror. He was the man immediately in charge of Black September, and therefore of the massacre of Israeli athletes at the 1972 Olympic Games in Munich.

In spite of what happened in Munich I can understand the great gains the PLO made by the use of violence at the beginning of their struggle. I can also understand their moral justification, or shall we say their argument for using violence, but what makes me angry is the way they do it, and that they do it now when it has outlived its purpose.

But when I was in Budapest, in spite of the fact that Abu Iyad had killed my people, I had the overwhelming feeling that if I only sat there and thought how bad he was, or how cruel he was or what injustices he did (and he would think about how many injustices we did and they are no less than his), we would never try to touch each other as human beings. Whether I liked it or not, here was a leader of the people I want to make peace with.

In the long, four-hour meeting we discussed all kinds of political issues. I tried to introduce the human element into our debate. I touched on some of what we are talking about here, and mentioned some of my own personal experiences. I could see that he was affected by this, and he began to talk about his childhood and his experience with Jews. This created a warm, electrical interchange.

That does not mean that I approve of what he is doing, but if I were to be the one to negotiate with him, I think I could do it. Is it trust? I don't know. To some of my friends on the left wing of Peace Now, I would say that there is one thing we should not forget: never mix up roles. They are Palestinians; they have their own interests and position in life. We are

Israelis and have our own political interests. That does not mean that we cannot compromise, but we both must keep our own identities. Only by remembering who we are can we communicate and find a way towards conciliation.

Why was I involved in all these things? I am convinced that eventually we have to make peace with the Palestinians. Therefore, we should not for a moment forget that they are human beings, and that they will be our neighbours with whom we want to live in peace. We should not do anything which may destroy that possibility.

* * *

My name is Bar-On, but it used to be Braun because my parents came from Germany. When you write it in Hebrew you only add a hyphen and then it means the "son of strength". In the 1950s, my father was a government official and travelled abroad. At that time there was almost a requirement to "Hebrewize" your name, and that is how the German "Braun" became the Hebrew "Bar-On". You had to have a very prominent father or an uncle like Chaim Weizmann not to be pressured to change your name.

I was born in Tel Aviv, but I grew up in a small place south of Tel Aviv called Rishon Lezion where there was a famous winery. Now it has become a sizeable town, but when I was there it had only 6000 inhabitants and was surrounded by Arab villages.

My mother was born Roman Catholic and my father was Jewish. Since my father was a Zionist, they thought it would be much better to create a completely new life in a different place rather than trying to decide questions about who they were and how to raise the children, so in 1924 they left Germany and came to Palestine.

I went to school in Rishon Lezion. There were rarely any Jewish/Arab mixed schools. Some children who went to British or missionary schools might have been educated with Arab children. There were mixed schools in Haifa and maybe in Jerusalem, but not in Rishon Lezion. There was a lot of mixing in the streets, however. Arabs would come to our homes and we would go to theirs, but we did not go to school with them.

My childhood was relatively quiet. Rishon Lezion was a little agricultural town with citrus groves and vineyards. I knew everybody, and had a very strong sense of security about who I was and what I was doing. I also happened to have a very good family. My mother was a very special woman.

Our family was secular but slightly traditional in a religious sense. We children grew up as non-believers. It wasn't that my father taught us not to believe, but rather that all three of my brothers and I participated in Hashomer Hatzair which was a secular, Marxist youth movement. However, my mother was a believer. She believed in God and maintained basic Jewish customs. My father made the prayer on Friday evening and on all the holidays. He would take us to the synagogue a few times a year, but the message we got at home was not one of doctrine or any kind of obligation to do this or that, but rather one of continuity and tradition.

I have continued traditionalism in my own family. Every Friday evening there is a prayer, and we celebrate all the holidays in the traditional way. I'm also very fond of the Bible and the traditional Jewish scriptures, so for me it is very important.

You may wonder how I can pray if I don't believe. I do not believe that there is a God who supervises and monitors us, but I very enthusiastically believe in the notion of holiness, in the ability of the human being to marvel at the world. I also believe that while the deities that are common now are creations of human culture, the fact that so many millions of people have for so many thousands of years believed in God makes him alive and true.

All my life I have made an effort to link myself with those people who do believe, because the fact that they believe and I don't is not what is important. What is important is that God exists in history and in the minds of people. Therefore, it is beyond what one person thinks; God is collectively there and because of that, I have to relate to him.

* * *

Our parents did not have to tell us anything about Arabs because until 1948 our relationships with them were on a day-to-day basis. For years an Arab woman named Aziza came to our house to do the washing. If you can think of the least bigoted and prejudiced person in this world, that was my mother. She approached every human being as an equal. My mother loved Aziza and that rubbed off on me. I spoke some Arabic; Aziza spoke some Hebrew so we could communicate. For a child that was enough, I did not have to talk philosophy or politics with her.

That was the situation in our house, but in addition there were many Arabs who lived in the community, workers at some orchards who lived in the courtyard, and those who came every morning to the market place to buy and sell. We met Arabs daily, we interacted with them, and we got to know some of them personally.

On the other hand, there was the problem of security and of the armed Palestinian as an enemy. From a very young age we didn't have to be taught that. For example, when I was about ten years old, we were living next to the wine cellars which very big and deep. I was sitting in my room doing some homework, and I heard a group of people running towards the cellars in a panic. There were about forty people, mostly elderly, and mostly new arrivals from abroad. I opened the window and asked what was happening, and they shouted back: "Jews are being killed in the orchards by the Arabs!"

It turned out later that indeed one Jew had been killed and it was someone I knew. But when these newcomers heard about it, they panicked and wanted to hide in the cellars. We used to call this kind of behaviour the "pogrom syndrome". I remember that I wondered why they felt they had to hide because after all we were in our own homeland and well defended by the Haganah, so there was no real danger.

Sometimes I think about this experience today when I see Israelis who continue to live the experience of the early Zionists. They still think they are in the early 1930s, and that the challenge is to win more land so the Jews can establish Jewish sovereignty — as if it does not already exist. They say that the whole country is theirs, and if the worst comes to the worst, they can chase everybody out. They have to understand that we already have a state and should stop being early Zionists and start becoming later Zionists.

* * *

From very early childhood we were aware that Arabs like Aziza and those we met in the street would be very friendly, but in principle they were members of a community that clashed against us, that did not want us to develop and occasionally would do violent acts against us.

In 1936 I was eight years old, and that was the beginning of three years of rioting by Arabs against the British and the Jews. We got newspapers every morning and I wouldn't really read them, but I saw pictures and the black-rimmed announcements about people who had been killed by mines or sniping or some other kind of attack. This kind of thing went on day in and day out, so it was no wonder that our relationships with Arabs took place within a complete dichotomy of defence, security and enmity on the one hand, and simple human interaction and, at times, even friendship on the other.

* * *

Now I am happy to say that at least in one case, my relationships with Arabs are real relationships. My second daughter is married to a Palestinian Arab, a Muslim whom I love. It always sounds strange to say that, but really he is one of the nicest persons I have ever met and I love him dearly.

* * *

I finished high school in 1946 but four years before, when I was 14, I was drafted to the youth battalions of the Haganah. It was an underground organization, but we were not yet handling weapons. We were trained with sticks and knives and later on, of course, also with revolvers and finally with larger guns.

Being a soldier and being drafted or volunteering for the army which defended the Jewish community was a very natural thing. Especially in a small place like ours, everybody was in some military organization. There were a few who were in Menachem Begin's group, the Irgun, but very few in our village.

After you volunteered for one or two years of military service, you would go to the Palmach which meant going to some kibbutz. I didn't go because at that time I was the head of the local chapter of my youth movement, and the headquarters in Tel Aviv demanded that I remain at home to continue this work.

Instead I volunteered to join a semi-legal police unit called the Jewish Settlement Police Force. We were given weapons by the British and were in uniform, so outwardly we were part of the British establishment, but really we were part of the Haganah. We got our orders from the Haganah, not from the British. On 30 November 1947 when the first skirmishes of the independence war started, I was still in this unit, and without any interruption I moved into the recently organized Israeli army.

Since I was a member of Hashomer Hatzair, I was supposed to join a kibbutz, but by October of 1948 I was already a company commander in the middle of one of the worst battles in the south. In the middle of the shelling I received a letter inviting me to the first gathering of my kibbutz.

I never made it to the kibbutz because I spent the next 22 years in the army.

Even though I didn't become a kibbutznik, for a while I still supported some of the Hashomer Hatzair ideology which advocated the establishment of a bi-national state in Palestine composed of both Jews and Arabs. Later I realized that a bi-national state was not a realistic possibility, and for pragmatic reasons we had had to accept partition as the solution. At the time, however, I never liked that solution, and thought we should have tried harder to have a bi-national state.

By April/May 1948, the image was very clear: the Arabs were the enemies, they were on the other side of the line and we were fighting them. There was this very deep sense of righteousness on our part because we had wanted to live peacefully. Maybe this feeling was more among Hashomer Hatzair than others because of our attempts to create a bi-national state. When that failed and the Arabs rejected the partition plan, we felt the war had been imposed on us by what we thought then was the intransigence or the stupidity of the Arabs. For that reason I had no problem fighting against the Arabs. Later on it was primarily against the Egyptian Army that I fought.

I killed Arabs. I killed not only in a blind way, some I killed almost personally. For example, during the truce between the two independence war campaigns, I was in charge of guarding one part of the demarcation line, and some of the Palestinians who had been chased out or had fled from some of the villages which were now on our side of the line would go back and try to reap the wheat or take some fruits. That was dangerous because they got accustomed to going back and forth and I was ordered to stop them on that section of the border.

We would ambush them, and in one of these ambushes there was a whole convoy of camels and donkeys coming back across the border from where they had taken their fruit or whatever. There were two or three men in front of the caravan making sure that the road was clear, and when I rose up to stop them, one man was only a yard away from me. Later on we found out that he was not armed, but I did not know that at the time.

He embraced me because he wanted to be close enough not to be shot, and I had to shoot him with my revolver. I killed him at very close range because he was almost on top of me, and I was frightened that he was attacking me.

* * *

This was the war. It did not in any way make me angry or hateful. I don't remember myself being angry with the Arabs until rather recently when some of the acts of terror have really upset me. I continue to belong to the camp that believes in conciliation and am ready to talk to the PLO, but I really feel that some of these incidents are unnecessary, stupid, and of course cruel.

I lost a nephew in the Yom Kippur War and I knew many people on our side who died in the wars, but I don't remember myself being especially angry or hateful about that. When I was the chief education officer of the Israeli army I made it a point to explain to the soldiers that hatred means fear and fear is a weakness we do not need. I made a pointed effort to educate the soldiers against hatred.

If you ask me how my commitment to peace showed itself in army service, I can tell you that, especially when I was the chief education officer, it certainly coloured my whole approach to how I thought the soldiers should be educated.

For example, in 1956 there was a massacre when 43 Arabs were killed by a group of Israeli soldiers in one of the villages on the old Green Line. The soldiers were arrested and they pleaded not guilty on the ground that they had only been obeying orders. The judge did not accept this excuse and they went to jail for many years. In his verdict, the judge stated as a general principle that in the Israeli army a soldier is obliged to refuse orders that are blatantly illegal. Now the term "blatantly" is important: here he meant something that is clearly illegal and as such, the soldier should and must disobey.

When I came to the army's eduction department in 1961, I had this verdict published in thousands of pamphlets so that every soldier would understand it. However, I had many fights about this with officers, especially those in the paratroops who were very rough and politically right-wing.

I remember I had a big fight with one of the chiefs of staff when a commander issued a pamphlet which included all kinds of chauvinistic, almost racist, terms about Arabs. When I saw it, I said it had to be banned and taken out of circulation, but the commander wouldn't do it. I went to the chief of staff and after a long fight, it was taken out of circulation.

* * *

We must remember that the whole story does not begin with the occupation of the West Bank and Gaza. The PLO was not established in

1967, it began in 1965 with the specific purpose of throwing me out of Tel Aviv, Jerusalem, or Haifa. The problem is that until today, it has failed to convince the majority of Israelis or the rest of the world that it has actually changed that aim.

Fortunately, I think the Israeli Arabs and most of the Palestinians in the West Bank are now ready for conciliation. They want peace and are ready for it. The trouble is that they cannot speak for themselves. They say that because they are occupied, we have to negotiate with the PLO who are outside the occupied territories and thus free to negotiate. I can understand this argument, but I know for sure that if they had their way, they would express their readiness to forget about old grudges and make a compromise on the basis of final arguments for conciliation. On that basis I am ready to conciliate.

Right now there are grounds for being pessimistic. If you only think of the prospects for peace in the situation as it is now, you can hardly be optimistic. Everyone talks about where the borders should be and what we are going to do with Jerusalem, but to my mind this is ridiculous because we don't have the basic condition for peace which is the honest desire on both sides to make compromises.

I mentioned my Palestinian friends who have started to understand, but the PLO is not yet there. Nor is the Israeli leadership. So what we have to think about are not overall solutions, but rather how we Israelis can transform ourselves — not the Palestinians but ourselves — to gain the clear political majority necessary to compromise.

The trouble is that we affect each other. I wish the PLO would use less violence and be more responsible with its rhetoric. If they did that, I would be more successful in my work. I guess if I could create a government with only Peres and not the Likud, it would be better for them too. It is a vicious circle.

What I have to do is influence and try to change Israeli attitudes. I also have to convey to the PLO leadership my honest feeling that they too have to change if they want to achieve even their minimum goals. There is no way for them to do this via America or the Soviet Union; the only way for them to achieve anything is by changing the hearts of the Israelis, and if they understand that, I am a real partner with them because that is my goal too.

The work on my side is educational work. I must convince the Israelis that there is a very high price for occupation, and while we may not readily see it now, the occupation is putting us in terrible danger in terms of our own interests. I have to make Israelis understand that the need for conciliation is not only a moral need, it is an existential one for both sides. They must understand that this land is a land of two nations, and the only viable solution is partition and conciliation.

We have to get out of the West Bank and Gaza. It is not a question of civil rights, it is a question of national rights. Occupation, even if benevolent, is inhuman. You can try to cause less pain, but that is not the point. The point is to work for a final settlement of our conflict and the eventual evacuation of those areas.

* * *

To ask for forgiveness does not necessarily include repentance. If I ask you for forgiveness, it means that I am aware that I did something wrong. Even if I know that by the very fact that I "was", that because I existed in a certain place, wrong was done to you, I still want to ask for your forgiveness even though the wrongs were wrongs that I could not avoid.

Of course both sides have done a lot of bad, criminal things to each other, but on the whole I cannot and I do not want to repent for the Zionist project. I can give you a whole lecture about why I think Zionism was justified, but even supposing the Zionist project was wrong, so what? I had no way of avoiding that wrong because I was born in this country. There is nothing in me that could have prevented my doing the things I have done: from fighting, from killing Arabs, or from participating in the Israeli army for 22 years and wanting to defend the state of Israel. It's an existential matter, and therefore I have no way of repenting and I don't want to repent. If I had to go through all of this again, I would do the same things.

I am, however, fully aware of a very important element in peace-making; it is that a basic wrong was done to the Palestinians. They suffered from the fact that we Jews returned to this place. They paid a high price that they shouldn't have had to pay, but couldn't help but pay. Therefore, I know that if and when they will accept that I cannot be but who I am, a Zionist living a Jewish existence in this land, then I will go down on my knees and ask for their forgiveness because they deserve it, and I think that is the only way they will ever realize that I did what I did because I had to.

Raja Shehadeh

Raja Shehadeh, 35, is a lawyer and author. He is a co-founder and current director of Law in the Service of Man, a West Bank human rights organization associated with the International Commission of Jurists in Geneva.

Shehadeh was educated at Bir Zeit University, and the American University in Beirut where he earned a degree in literature and philosophy. He studied law in England, and is a barrister of law and a member of Lincoln's Inn.

As an author, Shehadeh is most well known for his book, Samed — Journal of a West Bank Palestinian, *published by Adama Books, New York.*

Shehadeh comes from a distinguished family of jurists and writers. His maternal grandfather was a judge, and his uncle and father shared a law practice in Ramallah. In December of 1985 Shehadeh's father was murdered on the sidewalk in front of his house. To date, no suspects have been arrested.

I am a lawyer and I live and work in a place where there is no law. It is a frustrating and difficult life, filled with people who take the law into their own hands and cannot be stopped. The courts are in disarray, there is rampant injustice and you don't know who to turn to. Sometimes I dream about having the means to work properly towards creating a society where there is respect for people's dignity, rights and privacy.

Now the most difficult thing here is the lack of security. Of course, I have had an extremely bad experience, but generally it is the same for everyone: if it's not murder or robbery, it's interference in one's life. There is an absence of police; if you call them, they just won't come. We are in the strange situation of having an excess of army and an absence of police, and that is why life is so full of bad surprises. You always feel insecure, not because you can be taken and shot, but on a more ordinary level you can be murdered, and the murderer will never be found. You can be harassed and there is nobody here to protect you.

In every society there are people who exceed the limits, so imagine what it's like when you are living in a situation where the people in power cannot possibly care less about anything unless it affects their preoccupation with their own security. Anything that may harm the local Palestinian population doesn't bother them. If it has to do with taking away a bomb that could harm Israelis, that is one thing, but anything that has to do with the safety of the local Palestinian community... well, they can just go to hell. And we do go to hell. It's a very, very difficult time.

* * *

After the 1948 war when my parents left their home in Jaffa for Ramallah, the feeling was that this was only a temporary situation, and it would be just a matter of time before they would go back to Jaffa.

My parents left Jaffa because they knew they had no way of protecting themselves during the upcoming war. They knew, of course, about Deir Yassin and what had happened there, and they expected that there would be difficult times ahead because there was no Arab army to protect them.

They had a house here in Ramallah which they used in the summer because Jaffa is on the coast and it gets very hot. Since it was not going to be safe to stay in Jaffa, they thought it would be wiser to go to Ramallah and wait there until things became quiet, and then move back. But of course they were never allowed to go back.

When I was growing up in Ramallah, our house happened to face west and since the spot was quite high, we could see the lights of Jaffa at night. I grew up with the feeling that life in Jaffa had been much better than what we were experiencing in Ramallah.

* * *

Before 1967 we had absolutely no contact with Israel. Of course there was a lot of censorship, and because we didn't get any news, we were really left in the dark. Our only contact was my father's sister in Akko who had stayed on there during the war.

When they were allowed, she and the family used to come for a visit at Christmas. They would come for two or three days, and I remember that they would be in a very bad state, really shaken up. Of course I was young, but my general impression was that they were coming from some kind of battlefield. They looked like victims, exhausted and haggard. They could not bring many things with them when they came to us, and they seemed to think that our life here was much better and even materially more prosperous than theirs, though we really did not have very much.

Sometimes they said confusing things. For example, that there were great differences between life in Israel and where we lived, that the Jews were much more hardworking and were doing things that were not done here. There was some kind of mystique created which was never explained, and they seemed to be holding something back. I think they were genuinely worried about speaking. I don't know if that fear was well founded, though it certainly could have been, but I always had the sense that they were keeping something back, and it was not quite clear to us what life was like on the other side of the border.

* * *

Just before the 1967 war there was a lot of excitement in the air. Everyone was excited by Nasser's pan-Arab thinking, and the students in my school, especially those coming from the outside, were excited over the prospect of war. They were writing anti-American slogans on the walls and getting carried away with the excitement, and so was I.

Somehow, I thought that since war was such a long-awaited thing it obviously meant victory. There was no question in my mind: war meant victory. I felt a little uneasy that I could not participate in the war and the victory, but that was impossible because I was only 16 years old.

Then, I remember, we began to feel the effects of the preparations for war. There were warnings about what should be done, and then school stopped. After that everything seemed to rush, rush, rush.

Just before the war an old friend of my parents came and told us that he wanted to show us something, so we went with him to one side of Ramallah and were looking towards Jerusalem. The hostilities had already begun, and in a monotone he said that this war was going to be a repetition of 1948; it was not going to be a real war at all. He said the Israelis were going to take over the area just as easily as they had taken the other part of the country. Of course, I hated him for this. I don't think any of us, even my father, believed him. We didn't want to believe him so we didn't believe.

The war started, but in Ramallah we had almost nothing of it. Some planes dropped a few bombs, but we had absolutely no feeling of the presence of the Jordanian army. None of us, friends or family, had any acquaintances who participated in any way. We all stayed at home and waited. First, we heard all these false reports claiming Arab victories, and then after the second day we heard that the Israelis were in Jerusalem. On the third day they came to Ramallah and took over the Grand Hotel for their headquarters. That was it. That was the beginning of the occupation.

It was a shock and I didn't know how to take it. I was completely unprepared for meeting Israelis, and I couldn't appreciate what it would mean. The only fear came when people from the Latrun villages came walking with their belongings, and they told us that the Israelis had killed their men so I thought that Latrun was first and Ramallah would be next.

That night, the Israelis went around the town shooting, shooting, shooting, just to see if there was any resistance. There was none, but we did not know that. We sat in the house and tried to avoid the windows to protect ourselves from the bullets. I think that was the most scary time for me because as the shooting got closer, I expected the Israelis would get to our house, open the door and shoot us all. But that didn't happen.

Then there was no school. There was curfew, curfew, curfew. At that stage in my life it was very difficult because curfew meant being stuck at home. You could not move out of your house. I remember one time I went from the house to the garden and was going back in when a soldier at the Grand Hotel, which was right near where we lived, pointed his gun at me. I thought he would shoot because I was in the garden and not in the house. We couldn't even sit on the balcony.

* * *

After the war my parents had Israeli friends who came to visit, and we went to visit them in Israel so I had the chance to be exposed to various kinds of Israelis, especially civilians. That was a unique situation because the experience of most people, until now, has only been with soldiers. The soldiers tried to stay away, but if you went into the street you would meet them. If you went to Jerusalem, you were stopped at the roadblock.

Some Israelis tried to use the relationships they had with us to prove that since we had Israeli friends, we liked the occupation. There were also people who tried to misuse friendship in order to help ease their consciences about being occupiers. But there were others who wanted to help because they thought our family must be having difficulties after the occupation.

Now, after knowing a number of Israelis, I realize that they are not all alike and one has different experiences with them. There are some with whom you cannot get anywhere because you immediately disagree on facts.

For example, there are the Israelis who deny that there were ever any Palestinians in this land. That is nonsense. By saying that, they are denying my existence, so further communication is impossible. Unfortunately, you still do meet such people, and they argue so strongly that it seems their whole existence depends on being able to deny me mine.

There are Israelis who are completely in the mould of the fighter and say: "We won, we are still winning. This is our relationship — winner and vanquished — and therefore this fact will determine our relationship." By saying this they deny my humanity, and I cannot talk to them either. Strangely enough, these people, especially in shorter encounters, are unable to look me in the eye. It seems that if they do, they fear they will have to recognize my humanity, and that would throw them off balance. They see only what they want to see. Palestinians are only objects to be harassed, shot at and killed — all in the name of security.

There are times when I am very angry with my Israeli friends and think that because of what I am suffering in their name, they should completely disassociate themselves from Israel, Zionism... the whole thing. I just cannot tolerate their position. Yet dealing with these difficult issues together makes one realize, sooner or later, that there is suffering on both sides. This conclusion strengthens the friendship, and while it is certainly not easy, I think that the more complex a relationship is, the more satisfying it becomes.

Finally, there is the last group. I think it is wrong to put all of these people in one group, but I think what gives them some unity is that they are the people who are sensitive to the situation and are struggling with it. They don't unquestionably accept what they have been told about this situation, and they don't avoid difficult situations.

Having known these people, I sometimes think it is easier to be a Palestinian than an Israeli because for us it is all more clear-cut; we know exactly what is wrong. For an Israeli, it is not so easy. They do suffer from genuine fear, but at the same time, if they are real Labour Zionists and not Gush Emunim types, it is difficult for them to reconcile their humanism with their Zionism.

It's an extremely thorny question for them because they feel helpless. Things seem to be out of their hands, and they are also concerned about what's happening to their lives because of the growing extremism in Israel. They worry about the intolerance and the change in the quality of life, which may get to a such a point that it will be impossible for them to continue to live there. They want to do something, but they are not always sure what they can do. The question of civil disobedience, for example, becomes a very difficult one. They can't bring themselves to refuse to serve their army reserve duty in the West Bank, but at the same time they can't serve in the West Bank with a good conscience.

* * *

For Israelis there is a security in fear. Some people have had very difficult lives because they could not adjust to the possibility of a new attitude developing between Jews and Palestinians. They have very definite attitudes about who Palestinians and Jews are, and when they realize that things could be otherwise and perhaps the reality of the situation is other than what they have been taught, they just cannot change their attitudes.

Most people are not courageous, and they like security even if it is a security based on fear. Individual attempts to change attitudes do help and sometimes prove to be the seeds for something much more, but I, for one, have despaired of some of this because while positive things are happening, so many negative things continue to happen. Every day our situation in the West Bank is creating more of a separation between people. There is total separation between the West Bank settlers and the local Palestinians because both groups are unwilling and unable to accept the other.

Considering their arrogant vigilantism and the amount of Palestinian land that has been confiscated, I am totally unwilling to have anything to do with the West Bank settlers. I can accept Israelis living within the Green Line, but not the West Bank settlers. That is just out of the question.

* * *

I have experienced no dramatic turning points about how I view the situation here. I think it is because after I came here to work, I found it to be a very different experience from being a student. I was searching for a better understanding of what was happening around me, how I would deal with it, and what position I would take.

More than anything I wanted to be involved in building a better life for the people here. Since my training was in law, I wanted to work to improve the legal situation, and to improve people's awareness of and support for the rule of law. I began working in human rights and my idea of "samud", which in Arabic means steadfastly staying put and not leaving this land, is important because I believe that if we want to have a better life, we have to be the authors of that life; it is not going to come to us in a basket from the sky.

I think I grasped the idea of "samud" quite early, but it took me a long time to realize what it really means and how much suffering it involves.

It also took a while before I realized how thankless this work is. Considering that we live under a military government, I can't expect our human rights situation to be anything other than what it is. If our society was at the stage where there was fairness and everyone had their rights, then the work I am doing would be unnecessary. Naturally I understand that, but sometimes it is very difficult to come to terms with it emotionally. I have to remind myself constantly that I shouldn't expect what I am working for to become a reality. I just can't expect that to happen now.

* * *

At this point in my life, I am not a religious person. I started that way; I don't know how it was because my family is not necessarily religious. I know I have been influenced by Christianity, though, and I am amazed how it comes to me at certain points.

A few days ago I was thinking about this when I was meeting with a group of Arabs whom have been placed in power by the military authorities. Now they are acting very harshly towards other Arabs who I am trying to protect. As I sat listening to them, I thought how only the weak seem to get at the weak. To be magnanimous and generous, you have to be strong.

Then I realized how Christ had completely turned the tables, and showed how the weak could be strong and generous by forgiving. The act of forgiveness carries a lot of power. It is an assertion of one's dignity to have the means and ability to forgive. So Christ really did turn the tables around.

It may be difficult to understand, but idealistically speaking, I think that if there is to be peace here, there has to be forgiveness. Without question we Palestinians, through no fault of our own, have suffered for what happened to the Jews. I understand and feel strongly about the Holocaust, but I had nothing to do with it; I am not a European. They have suffered on account of something we had no part in. One can understand the need for the Jews to have a homeland. But if we are to come to terms with the Israelis, forgiveness will be required. We have to forgive them for what they did to us. They have also suffered and are suffering now. They have had many people killed in wars, and are having a difficult, insecure life. It may be fear that they themselves generate, but that doesn't matter. They are afraid because they have suffered.

Israelis also must forgive if there is going to be peace. The problem is that arrogance stands in their way, and I think they will have to lose some of this arrogance before they can see things differently. Now, if people offer them something they say, "Ah, good. Thank you", and take more. I hope they won't be forced to shed their arrogance through more bloodshed, but maybe that's the only way it will happen.

Hanna Siniora

Among the Palestinian leaders who live in the occupied West Bank,
Hanna Siniora *is one of the best known. For the past 12 years he has
been associated with the East Jerusalem Arabic newspaper,* al-Fajr,
*which is recognized as one of the main vehicles for expressing Palestinian
views. Currently Siniora is the paper's editor-in-chief.*

*In 1985 Siniora was one of two Palestinians chosen by Yasir Arafat and
accepted by the Israelis to be part of a proposed Jordanian-Palestinian
negotiating team. Later the peace process stalled and negotiations did not
take place.*

*Considered one of the leading Palestinian moderates, Siniora believes
that peace will only come when both Israelis and Arabs realize that the
disputed land must be shared. "If I want to find a solution for my own
problem," he says, "I have to think of the other party too. That is why I
realize that the only and best solution is for both sides to share the same
homeland."*

My family is a Jerusalemite family which has existed here for many
centuries. We have in the family Christians, both Greek Orthodox and
Roman Catholics. Part of the family has roots in Lebanon.

I was born in West Jerusalem and went to a Roman Catholic school
called Brothers College, just inside the Old City at the New Gate. My
father went there, I went there, and my son is now there, so it is a family
tradition.

I finished high school in Jerusalem in 1955, and went to the United
States to study engineering. I guess I did that because I wanted to rebel
against the family. My family has a pharmacy in the Old City, and
traditionally I should have taken over the business from my father, but at
that time I did not want to study pharmacy.

I started studying engineering in California at a junior college, then I went to Detroit to continue my study. After three years I decided that I had to go back home and study pharmacy. For a while I worked in the family business, and then went to the American University in Beirut and finished two years of pharmacy studies there.

Because of demonstrations and political upheavals at the American University (it was the end of the United Arab Republic), students were dismissed, and I had to come back and work again in the family business. Finally I finished my pharmacy studies in India.

In 1967 I was here during the summer vacation, and I saw our country taken over by the Israelis. None of the Palestinians fought because the government of Jordan did not trust us and we were unarmed.

After a month, I had to go back to school. At that time things were not formalized after the occupation of the West Bank, and people who wanted to leave for Jordan had to sign at the Allenby Bridge that they were going and not coming back. I thought: "Okay, I'll go to the university in Jordan, and after a full academic year the Israelis will have withdrawn and things will be normal again. Then I'll come back home so I don't have to worry." So I signed that I was not coming back.

Fortunately for me I was married and my wife stayed here. She was able to organize a family reunion, and asked the authorities to allow me back so I was able to get back to Jerusalem. In 1969 I came to live permanently here, and started back in the pharmacy business.

* * *

I had a cousin, Mr Nasr, who started this newspaper in 1971. He was kidnapped in 1974, and his sister came over from the United States and we tried to find out his fate. At that time we hoped that we could find him or that he would be released. Later on, after a few years, we found out that he was murdered the same night he was kidnapped and until today we have never seen his body.

So the sister told me: "You are the nearest member of the family who can look after the paper until my brother comes."

I said: "Okay, I will do it. I don't know anything about journalism, but I will look after the business side, and as soon as your brother shows up he can take over."

For the past 12 years I have been caretaker of the paper. I started in the business side, but found that I liked journalism much more than being a pharmacist. Now I really am quite involved in this new career of mine, and it has also got me into politics.

* * *

I have strong feelings about my Palestinian identity and yet I feel that we all — Israelis and Palestinians alike — are human beings. So if I want to find a solution for my own problem, I have to think of the other party too. That is why I realize the only solution is for both sides to share the same homeland, because we have one homeland and are two national movements.

In my opinion, then, the only alternative is for us to understand that both parties have to make mutual concessions. We have to partition this land. In this way, we can create stability and develop peace and understanding. Probably many generations later both our peoples will develop the dynamics that are now becoming a fact of life in Europe, where nationalism has subsided and there are economic relationships and understanding between all of the Western European countries. Borders are becoming almost obsolete, and people move from one country to another.

I hope that this kind of thing will develop here between the Palestinians and Israelis, but it can only be done when there is parity between the two sides. Now there is no parity.

We are an occupied people. We are feeling the pressure. There is a consistent Israeli policy towards throwing us out of our country. It is being done very quietly by denying us opportunities to survive. Our land is being confiscated. Taxation policy is carried to the extreme in order to deprive us of a fair share of income, and we are not being allowed to develop independently our economic infrastructure. We are becoming nothing more than a captive labour pool for the Israelis.

Yet, we do not despair; we do not give up hope. We understand that the history of confrontation, violence, struggle, and wars has created a very tense situation. It has made us stereotype each other horribly. We have to work to change attitudes. I believe there is this realism on both the Palestinian and Israeli sides. I believe a majority of Palestinians have a realistic political attitude.

In Israel, the realists are a minority. However, I think they are a growing minority. This change in attitudes is an evolutionary process, and it will take some time. But we have to push it forward because if we don't, further calamities will befall each side and more wars will take place.

* * *

I abhor violence. I just don't believe in fighting it out. We have to reason it out. We have to have a principled understanding of the issues.

Maybe some of this kind of understanding can come from one's upbringing and schooling. I went to a French Catholic school which promoted an awareness of Christianity. At the same time, I believe that meeting people and getting in contact with various kinds of views and travelling abroad — all of this widens the perspective.

Studying, analyzing and understanding history shows that the policy of accommodation and mutual concession brings better results than imposing one's will on people. In all my actions and work I try to be persuasive and not coercive. Sometimes because of that I am accused of being weak and soft, but I'd rather find a solution that all the parties can live and be happy with, rather than impose a solution which will be set aside later.

* * *

My experience with Israelis really started in 1969, and at that time most Palestinians did not even dare to talk to them because we did not know or understand them. We had no dialogue with them at all. Also, we thought that associating or talking with Israelis might be a treacherous act.

I remember that we had a Palestinian neighbour who came from the Galilee, and he was working in the government here. For a whole year, we barely said "good morning". Then we started trying to talk to one another and visit, and slowly a good friendship developed. That was the beginning of unity between Palestinians within the Green Line and in the occupied territories.

This experience showed me how first impressions and attitudes can change. It also gave me the courage to begin developing contacts with the other side.

At the time I became a journalist one of my duties was to comment on the news, not emotionally but factually. And I began to form very good working relationships with many Israeli journalists, especially those who were covering the West Bank. I began to participate in some small dialogue groups with Palestinians and Israelis, and that was how my views gradually developed on the issues. Actually, when our paper first started, it was called *Hardline*, and didn't accept any political concessions. Gradually, with me mellowing the paper mellowed too.

* * *

I have become more and more aware that there is another way besides the military way. Gradually I adopted that outlook, and I try to explain it publicly to the Israelis. I want them to understand that we are a people with culture, with hopes, with aspirations, and that we are not terrorists. We don't want to throw them into the sea; we want to live in peace, side by side with Israel, and we should have a place we can call home as they have been able to have a place that they call home.

Because I feel this way, I have been able to work with my fellow Palestinians who agree with this, and I've built a good network with Israelis who also perceive that we should have our right to self-determination. This attitude has even drawn the attention of the Palestinian leadership.

I found out that Mr Arafat carries exactly the same views as I do. He is a man who wants to go down in history as a peace-maker. He is not perceived as such; people try to stereotype him as a terrorist, but all of his actions through the many years have been consistent. He has been trying slowly but surely to get his people to accept that they must make major concessions and change their mind about wanting to control all of the land. He wants them to accept a mini-state on 22 percent of the land, and considering what we had before, this is a big sacrifice. As a political leader he cannot make his people accept this at one stroke. He has to try very hard to instill this understanding in them, and it has been a hard fight all along.

* * *

There are some Israelis who understand the issues even better than I do, but because of political expediency do not want to accept us as a people. They covet our land and they don't want to share it with us even though they know that we have a more just claim to it than they do.

But there are also many Israelis who are really human beings. They feel they have to fight for the rights of others as they have been fighting for their own rights, and I tell you I feel really touched by those people. I believe that those people, who have this moral courage to fight for their principles, are going to be able one day to win their way and influence their people. This is the only way that both Palestinians and Israelis can make peace and survive and live as neighbours.

I always try to understand what makes the other side tick, and I have really felt that the Israelis have a major concern about their security. Their fear is that everybody is after them, that even their greatest ally, the United States, will one day desert them. Because of this fear they sometimes become boisterous and act arrogantly. "We can alone defend ourselves," they say, "and we don't have to rely on anybody; we have to appear tough, and should not let sentiment interfere with national security."

Both Israelis and Palestinians are human beings. They have fears, they have misconceptions, and they lack the ability to communicate. This accentuates the negatives on both sides. With more contact these misconceptions can be corrected, the fears can subside, and I realize that there are many, many Israelis — like there are many, many Palestinians — who want co-existence. Some of them are very outspoken about it and say: "What is good for us should be good for you."

I try to tell the Israelis that we also have our fears, and we see that they have designs not only on our future but on our land and our very survival. They try to justify their fears by saying: "Look, we have only a small part of the area under our control, and you have the whole Arab world. If you lose your home here, you can have it in Amman or Lebanon or Syria or Egypt."

But I remind them of the feeling that made them, for many thousands of years, yearn to come back here. Well, we have it too, and it is the driving force in the Palestinian community. We have to try to understand each other and overcome those fears. In every single public talk, I always say that we will especially listen to the security needs of Israel because I understand that they have this fear. It really is one of the factors that at this moment makes peace so difficult to achieve.

I think that politicians on both sides are doing us a great disservice. They try to outmanoeuvre the other side and, in this way, instead of making things more manageable and easier to resolve, they are creating an impossible problem. Mr Peres talks about peace and has been very successful in his public relations drive to convince the Western world that he wants peace, and that the Palestinian side, especially the PLO, is to blame for all the trouble.

But Peres has so dehumanized the PLO that now it is becoming almost impossible to sit down and find a solution. The Palestinian people say: "You want a solution and we want a solution... you have to talk to our leadership." But nobody will talk to our leadership. We really need a whole process of re-education in order to clean up this brainwashing that the Israeli political system has been carrying out about the Palestinian people, especially their leadership.

* * *

Honestly, many times I say "To hell with it", and just want to give up and maybe find something to do that is more consistent with my training as a pharmacist. Sometimes I just want to get out of this whole business of trying to change attitudes. But at the same time I feel that it is a driving duty for me. If I don't want to do it, who else will want to?

It's so much easier to be a strong nationalist rather than a peace-maker. It is easy to please the crowd by letting them hear what they want to hear. But to try to re-educate them, to try to make changes is so difficult. Sometimes many of the local leadership, and Mr Arafat too, are being called traitors because we advocate a sort of middle road.

We also have been brainwashing our own people into saying: "We want everything or nothing. This is the way and there is no alternative." So we are trying to change those attitudes on our side, as well as trying to impress upon the Israelis that they also have to change attitudes.

Our work has been so difficult because we have to face the extremist opposition and their sloganeering against us, and then at the same time face some of those Palestinian fringe elements who would even threaten us physically. Some of those threats have been carried out, so it's a difficult and very dangerous path. But it is a path that many have to take because this is the only way to change the present situation.

I always believe that I cannot ask the United States, or Great Britian or the Europeans or even our Arab neighbours, to make the changes and get us what we want. I have learned that a people has to rely on its own sons and daughters, and this is what I am perceiving right now within the Palestinian movement. The Palestinians are finally realizing that a solution has to come from within. They themselves have to work, and the first people to convince and change are not the Americans or the Europeans but our adversaries: the Israelis.

Really, we, the Palestinians, would like to live in peace and in equality with the Israelis. I would like the Israelis to know this. We have perceived that there is, at the moment, a Palestinian problem and we don't want to create a Jewish or Israeli problem in the future.

I believe in equality, and that is why I said that what is good for the Israelis should be good for the Palestinians. If we can respect and accept each other and mutually make concessions, then we are on the way towards achieving an understanding and finding peace. Otherwise, if there is the slightest misconception that this is just a grand design in order to destroy the other party, it will not work.

* * *

Well, you know there are ups and downs in all of this. But generally, I believe we are making headway even among a very difficult audience like the American Jewish community who are more conservative than the Israeli Jews here. I am finding out that there is a change in attitudes though it is very slight and slow.

We need the influence of the governments of the world, and I mean the big powers like the United States, the Soviet Union, Great Britain and France. They should also help change attitudes. I mean if these countries really want world stability, if they want to end nuclear confrontation, they have to work at peace-making more seriously, and that is why many times I accuse the Americans of having a foreign policy of "crisis management". They seem to accommodate the guy who can lobby the most and who has the most influence. This is not a policy of justice and equality. I believe it goes against the grain of the United States' constitution and the principles of the American people.

Am I an optimist or a pessimist? I believe that even in the darkest hours of our lives, we have to have hope, and I continue to have hope because I believe in the goodness of the human being. I believe there are fears and we have to address those fears, but basically, intrinsically, human beings are good and they want to live in peace. That is why I believe we have fertile ground to make headway in both camps. Both the Palestinians and the Israelis really yearn for peace; they want peace. It's the politicians who don't have the courage, and we have to keep prodding and working, and eventually we will win.

Simcha Flapan

*The Polish-born **Simcha Flapan**, 75, has been working for a peaceful settlement of the Israeli/Palestinian conflict for the past fifty years. After immigrating to Palestine in 1930 and settling in a kibbutz, he began dialogues with Arab intellectuals — a process that culminated in 1957 with the founding of* New Outlook *a magazine which Flapan edited until his retirement.*

The purpose of New Outlook *is to serve as a medium for the clarification of problems concerning peace and cooperation among all the peoples of the Middle East. Over the years, the magazine's pages have been filled with a wide variety of Jewish, Arab and Palestinisn opinion, all aimed at one thing: the elimination of frictions and animosities in the area.*

I came from a well-to-do family of Polish businessmen. I did not have a Jewish education because we lived in the west of Poland where there were only 300 Jewish families in a town of 100,000 people. There I realized the seriousness of national conflicts because both Poles and Germans lived in the town. There was a German minority of nearly 30 percent, and relations with the Poles were a problem. There was mutual hostility, fear and suspicion, and before the German army invaded Poland, the Poles organized a kind of pogrom upon the German community. Then when the Germans came in, they took vengeance and organized a pogrom on the Polish community.

The years before 1930 were times of very great economic and social crises in Poland. I visited my grandfather who was living in a Jewish town, and I saw misery, poverty, lack of employment, and anti-Semitism.

It was also a time when Jewish youth in Poland faced a choice because of the rising tide of communism. These young people were trying to decide whether or not to join the Communist Party. By joining they hoped not only to create a new social order, but also to solve the problem of anti-Semitism and discrimination. Their other choice was to join the Zionist movement which advocated the establishment of a Jewish society in Palestine. I can remember discussing this problem with my friends, and for a time I was not able to decide which way to go. In the end, I decided that the Jewish problem would not be solved by a social revolution in Poland because the prospects of such a revolution were very poor. The only way to bring revolution, I thought, was through immigration and the creation of a Jewish society, and that was why I joined the Hashomer Hatzair movement. They proposed that I go to Palestine, and when I arrived here I joined a kibbutz.

I knew that there were Arabs in Palestine and that there was a conflict, but because Hashomer Hatzair wanted to develop a bi-national state, I was not worried because I really thought this would be possible. In 1929 there had been very serious riots, and many Jews came back to Poland because of the riots. However, I believed in the possibility of setting up a common movement of Jewish and Arab workers which would lay the foundation for common living in Palestine. I regarded Palestine as a common homeland for the Jewish and Arab people.

Our kibbutz was surrounded by Arab villages. As a herdsman in the kibbutz I was meeting Arab herdsmen and I also had some clashes with them. Early in the 1930s I decided to go with a friend and talk to Arabs, and I remember we met all kinds of Arab notables and intellectuals in Nazareth. I tried to study the social and economic background of the conflict because it was not a purely national conflict.

Later, after the establishment of the state, I ran the Department of Arab Affairs of the Mapam Party for 11 years. There is hardly a village in Israel that I did not visit, and I established very close contacts with Arab intellectuals. I began to edit an Arabic newspaper, and together with my Arab friends founded the first Arab publishing house in Israel.

* * *

I was influenced by the Hashomer Hatzair movement which was not only one of the biggest youth movements in the diaspora, but also created the largest kibbutz movement in Israel.

Martin Buber was also an influence because when I began to run the Arab Affairs Office, I had connections with him. Together with his group we created a league for Jewish/Arab rapprochement in the late 1930s.

When I began to deal with the problems of the Arabs, Buber asked me to be in touch with him and to come once a month and tell him what was happening. He was interested not only in the theoretical aspects, but in practical things like the relations between kibbutzim and Arab villages. I saw him often, and from him I learned that the only way to find common understanding is by dialogue.

One of the results of our discussions was the founding of *New Outlook* magazine whose aim was a dialogue with the Arabs, both with Palestinians and the rest of the Arab world. We also hoped to give the Arabs objective information about what was going on in Jewish society and vice versa. As editor of *New Outlook*, I set up personal contacts with Arab intellectuals both in Israel and abroad. I travelled to Europe and the United States to meet with Arabs and discuss what could be done because I believed Buber was right when he said that if we didn't solve the problem, we would face a series of wars, each one more destructive than the other.

Most of my contacts were not with Palestinians because at that time they were not playing a large role as a national group. Their allegiance was to pan-Arabism because as a small people facing the thrust of Jewish colonization, they could not hope to win their case without the support of the whole Arab world. Later, I established relationships with Palestinian leaders, especially with two representatives of the PLO, Issam Sartawi in Paris, and Said Hammami in London. These contacts became deep, personal friendships, and although the idea was to discuss what could be done, many of our meetings were devoted to extremely long discussions of the past and the roots of the misunderstandings. As a result of those contacts, I came to the conclusion that in order to build a better future, we had to overcome the myths of the past.

I learned a great deal from Sartawi and Hammami before they were both assassinated. It was precisely their assassination that made me understand that only peace with Palestinians would pave the way for peace between us and the Arab world. I understood that they were not assassinated because they were marginal personalities. If they had lacked a constituency and the support of a large part of the Palestinian people, nobody would have cared about them. It was precisely because they represented a dynamic trend among Palestinians that they paid with their lives.

Issam Sartawi was a charming, intelligent person who was dynamic and full of imagination. You know, we say that politics is the art of the possible, but if you have more imagination, more things are possible. As an imaginative politician he was irreplaceable. It is interesting, though, that he did not start his political career with a strategy for peace. His first idea was to persuade the Arab governments to take back and absorb all the Jews from the Middle East who had come to Palestine. He went to all the Arab states trying to persuade them to make offers to Jews to come back and they would receive their houses and their property.

Soon, he discovered that this solution was unworkable and he began to establish contacts with the Israeli peace people. He went on to develop a very creative, imaginative strategy which produced great results.

He paid a price not only by losing his life, but his struggles for peace within the Palestinian movement also brought him a lot of trouble. For example, he was not elected to the PLO executive and sometimes he was socially isolated, but he never gave up his ideas and he fought for them courageously. He was not the first and he is not the last. There are quite a number of Palestinian leaders who continue to work in the same direction.

I had many discussions with him and we did not agree on everything. We had differences of opinion on tactics, but these differences existed within a very deep friendship, and in the end we always found some solution.

His death was a great loss to all of us working for peace, but he was only one of a new generation of Palestinians, and I believe the numbers of these people are growing. The danger is that if we do not reach some kind of a political solution in the next few years, there may be a rise of radical fundamentalism or pan-Arab, revolutionary tendencies. Now Israel is facing a choice: whether in the next two years to make an agreement with the Palestinian movement, which is now a secular, national movement, or watch the rise of fundamentalism in the whole Arab world, including among the Palestinians. If this happens, it will mean a much greater danger for Israel.

* * *

My fundamental approach to Arabs has not changed, but my ideas about the conflict have changed. Until 1970 I believed that Jordan could be the Palestinian state, that Palestinian self-determination could be realized in the framework of peace between Israel and Jordan. Until then I did not have much faith in the impact of the Palestinian movement. I felt that the best way to work out peace was to attach the conquered territories to Jordan. The turning point came in 1970 when King Hussein organized the war against the PLO and drove them out of Jordan. Then I understood that Jordan, too, had no future without the solution of the Palestinian problem and that the Palestinians — without a state, without a government, without an army — are the most important factor in peace-making because they are not a military threat to Israel. Certainly terrorism is causing a lot of tensions and troubles and is very annoying to the Israeli public, but the Palestinian people do not present a military threat to Israel. They *would* be a real threat if any attempt is made to make peace without solving their problems. Why? Because they can prevent every peace solution which ignores their national problem.

In my view the Palestinian problem is a new Jewish problem. Their strength comes from the diaspora, the aspiration to overcome their dispersion and have a national home of their own. This was the strength of the Zionist movement, and it is now the strength of the Palestinian movement. We can oppress them, we can defeat them militarily, we can occupy the West Bank and Gaza for a very long time, but we cannot eradicate from their hearts and minds the aspiration to be a free, independent and sovereign people.

The alternative choices for us are either co-existence with the Palestinian people or co-destruction. There is no other choice. We must solve this problem because only the Palestinians can introduce us to the Arab world. Egypt tried to do it, but Egypt isolated itself from the Arab world. It is only the Palestinians who live in the whole Arab world and play such an enormous role there who can help us. They provide not only the skilled workers, but the intellectuals, the lawyers, the teachers, the scientists, and sometimes even the politicians and diplomats. The Palestinians helped to build up the Arab states, but they were not assimilated into that world because they have always wanted to return and live in their own homeland.

The only solution is dialogue with the Palestinians and an agreement on the creation of a Palestinian state which will co-exist in peace with Israel. By the way, this was the decision of the United Nations in 1947 which we accepted: two states in Palestine within an economic union. So we are now coming back to it and I do not see any other solution.

* * *

Yes, I am a Zionist. You know, a friend of mine who works for the *Jerusalem Post* once wrote an article saying that he was a Zionist but also for a Palestinian state. I would say that I am for a Palestinian state because I am a Zionist, meaning that I am a Zionist because I believe people cannot live as national minorities in permanent dispersion and under discrimination. The desire to be independent and sovereign cannot be eradicated.

Certainly, there was a long time when Zionism was something the Arabs thought to be a kind of curse. Zionism was reactionism, racism, chauvinism — whatever you want. My main work has been to persuade my Arab friends that there is not just one Zionism; there are two Zionisms.

The first Zionism was not just a movement struggling for a Jewish state because there were Zionists like Martin Buber and those in the Hashomer Hatzair movement who were against a Jewish state. For them Zionism meant building a new Jewish society, a society with more justice, more equality, more human values — a better society.

At present there is a second Zionism dominating the minds of Israelis although I think that it is weakening a bit. For most Israelis this Zionism only means "a Jewish state". If you ask what kind of a Jewish state, they reply that it is not important. To them, Zionism means Jewish power by having a Jewish state controlling territory.

The first Zionism was the dominant force until 1948 and what has happened, especially in the last ten years, is that the second Zionism got the upper hand, and as a result Menachem Begin's Likud coalition came to power in 1977. The Labour government, which preceded Likud, prepared its own defeat by not emphasizing the social, moral and ethical values of Zionism. It preferred to focus on the territorial configuration of Israel after the big victory in the 1967 war. This was a major turning point in Israel's and the Zionist movement's history. After 1967 the intoxication of victory was so great that all the old tendencies for a "Greater Israel" were revived and this paved the way for Begin.

Now more and more people understand that we have a contradiction. Either we have a Jewish society based on the social values of equality, justice and socialism, or we can have a Jewish state oppressing another people.

* * *

Fear is understandable because of Jewish history and the Holocaust, but it is not a rational fear. It is not justified objectively because we cannot project upon the Arab world the traumas of the Holocaust. The Arabs did not organize and execute the Holocaust, and we are not a Jewish ghetto community encircled by a gigantic military power like

Germany. The objective relationship is quite different here in the Middle East. We are a military super-power vis-à-vis the Arab world, so the projection of our Holocaust fears upon the Arab world is completely unjustified. I do not, however, minimize the dangers because there are still Arabs who want another round of hostilities, but I believe that this trend has very few advocates because the Arabs, too, have begun to understand the enormous changes that have taken place in the Middle East. They know that another war would only lead to the destruction of all the people.

Both Israelis and Palestinians are schizophrenic. We both have a world of dreams and historical memories, but we also have developed a sense of pragmatism and realism. I will share with you one experience which I have repeated many times because it is very characteristic.

A very close Lebanese friend of mine and I were working in Paris between 1966 and 1968. One day we arranged a public meeting at which both of us were supposed to speak about peace. Well, that day he came to me in the morning to discuss the details and he told me: "Ah, I feel so happy today, I had such a nice dream."

"What was the dream?" I asked.

"I dreamt that Israel did not exist," he answered.

This was a real shock to me and I was terribly confused because I was supposed to go with him to the meeting, and I was trying to decide how I should react to his remark. Should I react to his dream, or should I react to the fact that we were going to speak about a peaceful solution? I decided that I should not react to the dream. Let him have his dream, I thought; we Jews also have our dreams. Some of us would be very happy if the Arab world would move away, but we live in reality and cannot change the geography. Because Israel will always remain in the middle of the Arab world, we have to forget the dreams and work for co-existence.

The Palestinians and the Arabs also have fears, but we Israelis have demographic fears: the Arabs have numbers and oil money and can buy the same weapons that we are buying, and there may come a time when they become so modernized and organized that our "blitz victories" will be out of the question. This is a real fear in Israel.

On the other hand, the Arabs fear Israel's supremacy in technology and science. Sometimes they have an exaggerated opinion of our supremacy. Our relationships, especially with the United States and the imperialist powers, make them fear that one day we shall rule the whole Arab world.

So the fears exist and to some extent they are justified on both sides. The problem is how to eradicate them. I believe this can be done, but what worries me is that there seems to be development in diverse directions. What I mean is that we Israelis started pragmatically: we accepted the United Nations' decision about two states in Palestine, and most of us renounced our vision of having the whole of Palestine become a Jewish national home. We accepted the partition for pragmatic reasons. Now the victories in the wars have strengthened our aspiration to have a "Greater Israel", and that is what gave rise to Begin and the Likud. The Arabs developed in the opposite way. They started with the view that as one of the largest populations in the world, they would be able to eliminate the small Israeli state, or at least dictate the terms of peace. Now the Arabs are developing in the direction of a more realistic appraisal of the situation. They know they cannot eliminate Israel because the military option does not exist. They must come to terms with the Jewish state, and their only condition is the solution of the Palestinian problem.

Sure, some Palestinian elements still talk about "armed struggle", but for all practical purposes they have given it up. There is resistance to the Israeli occupation, but this can be understood. However, the armed struggle is not a strategy determined by the leadership because they have come to accept the existence of Israel. As a matter of fact, the "Fez Plan" means recognition of Israel. Resistance is expressed by throwing stones and through isolated incidents of violence, but it is not an overall strategy of armed struggle any more. The Palestinians do not give up the right to an armed struggle because they believe that if all political attempts fail, they will have no other choice than to try it again. However, their concrete strategy is to seek a political solution.

* * *

I am hopeful. For fifty years I have been engaged in the search for peace, and I am still hopeful. I have to be. You know there is a Jewish joke: What is the difference between an optimist and a pessimist? A pessimist says: "It can't be worse." An optimist says: "No, it can be worse."

I am this kind of an optimist who is trying to prevent things from getting worse, because if things become worse it will be a disaster not only for the people in the Middle East but also for world peace. A new Sarajevo could happen in the Middle East. My optimism is based on the desire to prevent such a thing so that everything does not become worse.

Simcha Flapan died in April 1987. The following inscription, from Isaiah, has been placed on his tombstone: "Nation shall not lift up sword against nation, neither shall they learn war anymore."

Jeremy Milgrom

Jeremy Milgrom, a 33-year old American-born rabbi, admits that he lived in Israel for 14 years before becoming actively involved in the peace movement. As an Israeli army reservist, he was called up for the Lebanon war. However, believing that the war was "unjustly and undemocratically declared", he responded to the call-up by fasting and was eventually sent home.

From that time on, Milgrom has been involved in an organization called Yesh G'vul, meaning "There is a Limit". The "limit" refers to the organization's belief that there should be a declared limit to Israel's borders.

Yesh G'vul's original goal was to end the Lebanon war and provide support for those soldiers who refused to serve. Now the group's aim has shifted towards supporting soldiers who refuse to do reserve duty in the West Bank.

In addition to his work in Yesh G'vul, Milgrom teaches at Hebrew University, is active in interfaith dialogues, and serves a Conservative congregation in the town of Rehovot.

I went to elementary school in the state of Virginia, and every morning we recited the Pledge of Allegiance, sang the National Anthem, "Dixie", and finally "Carry Me Back to Old Virginia".

When I was eight years old our family went to Israel because my father, who is a rabbi, took a sabbatical year there. After I came back from Israel, I sang "Dixie" differently. I'd sing, "In Dixie Land I'll take my stand", but I wouldn't sing, "to live and die in Dixie". I thought that while I didn't mind living in Dixie, I should die in Israel.

* * *

I was 15 when I came to Jerusalem to study at a yeshiva. That year really turned me upside down in many ways because while my studies were challenging, they were also theologically disturbing. I was confronted with notions which I couldn't accept rationally and, being the son of a Conservative rabbi, I was bothered by the lack of theological alternatives. I was also away from my family, from my classical music and a lot of other familiar things. In one sense it was a period of sensory and emotional deprivation, but in another sense it was exciting because I was studying the classical rabbinic texts four or five hours a day and living Judaism with all its traditional ritual.

I do remember having this incredible love for the land and the people, something that still characterizes my feelings about Israel. There was the feeling that in every step I took I was walking over at least twenty levels of history. It made me wonder if any of my relatives had ever been in this place before. If you are a Jew, being here makes you feel very connected.

I would spend every free moment hiking with topographical maps, getting to know the land and feeling that I expressed ideology by physically becoming part of it. Only later did I discover that this romanticism is very dangerous because it means a shift in values that cannot but put other very important values in jeopardy.

On Friday nights the yeshiva students walked to the Western Wall to pray and dance. We came back through the Old City walking together in closed ranks with our arms around each other, still dancing and singing. What I wasn't aware of then, was how we walked in the street. We were charging up the street, and if anyone happened to be in the way, they had to move. What we were singing was from one of the minor prophets: "They have their vehicles and their horses", we sang, "but we go in the name of the Lord."

We sang that we had faith rather than weapons, but in reality we were the vehicles. We were like a wall, a phalanx, pushing our way through. Of course there were people in the way — the Arab residents of the Old City — and I remember seeing terror on some of those faces we shoved aside. There was something very incongruous about that; it was a kind of confrontation that I later realized was part of a pattern we had all got into.

In 1968, a friend of mine from the yeshiva tried to tell me that the Vietnam War was okay. It was a good war, he said, because it gave Israel the chance to buy weapons that had been tested in a real war. That really pushed me to the brink because I was totally opposed to the war. What he was really saying was that Jewish souls were worth more. Because we have a crucial role to play in the world's redemption, it's okay if our military might comes at the price of other people's lives. It was not only the theological statement that bothered me, it was also the political implications that I didn't want anything to do with.

* * *

Then, like almost every young Jewish man or woman in Israel, I joined the army. I volunteered because I wasn't yet a citizen. From then on my concerns were really practical, making sure that I had not misplaced my uniform, that I had enough food to eat, that my gun was clean so I could get home for the weekend and not be held back as punishment. In other words it was really mundane, tangible survival and I saw no combat. Luckily 1971-73 were peaceful years.

Before the Yom Kippur War broke out I had been trained as a paratrooper and was combat-ready, but in the meantime I had joined the air force. Since they didn't want to take the chance of wasting a future pilot, I didn't see any combat. That fact may have saved my life.

Meanwhile my classmates were dying left and right. During the spring and fall of 1974, I went to a succession of funerals. There were twenty boys in my section of the high school class, and three were killed in the war. They were all good friends, and they all died in tanks. A fourth friend was brain damaged. He functions okay, but he's a different person now. On the one hand I felt guilty for not having been in the war, but on the other I felt a great deal of relief at not having been part of it.

I couldn't stand the army, but my reserve duty was different because I was in a much more serious unit than my regular army unit. Most people do serious work in the real army, and they think reserve duty is nothing more than a waste of time. For me it was just the opposite because my reserve unit was a top-notch, anti-tank unit. We did all kinds of stuff that scared me, but I felt that if there was a job to do, why should someone else do it and not me?

The Lebanon war, however, was a war I didn't want to go to. It was a war I thought was unjustly and undemocratically declared, and I was against it from the beginning. It seemed as though we were just picking a fight.

My collar bone had been broken in a bicycle accident, and because I was still being medically reclassified, I was not called into Lebanon when the war broke out. When I was finally called up, I tried my hardest to find an alternative posting, and ended up just south of the border.

But finally I was called into Lebanon. Though it was a hard choice, I decided to serve the week or ten days rather than refuse and land in jail for a month. I went up hoping to convince the commander to let me go, but as soon as we crossed the border I realized that I had no chance of convincing him of anything; I was just part of the herd.

I was feeling very disappointed in myself. I knew this war was bad, and that the best way to fight it was to refuse to go, even if I had to go to jail. But here I was, hungry and tired, in Lebanon. When I got to the base I decided that I would begin my defence; I would just stay within that force-field of hunger, fatigue and non-compliance. I didn't want to antagonize anybody so I went to the officer in charge and said: "I'm here by accident."

"None of us want to be here," he said.

"Well," I said, "I can't look after myself, and I can't be of any help to you either."

"What do you mean?" he asked.

"I'm not going to eat or drink," I answered.

That thought had just occurred to me twenty minutes before, and I decided I wasn't going to budge from it. I decided that simply refusing to function would be more effective than anything political I could say.

Well, that raised some eyebrows. After about two days of fasting, they sent me home. I was relieved and strengthened because it was the first time I had ever been able to stand up to the army and say no.

When I got back to Israel I really felt cut off. The army had been so much a part of my identity, it was where my friends were, and it was part of my belief in the state of Israel.

Since my self-esteem and sense of worth were suspect, I converted these feelings into action by getting very involved with Yesh G'vul, the only group that supported draft resistance during the Lebanon war.

Those of us who resisted going to Lebanon really put our reputations on the line. We faced a lot of ostracism, rebuke and ridicule. It's not like in the US where none of your friends go to the army. Here, when all your friends are going and the border is so near, conscientious objection raises a lot of questions and makes people feel insecure.

Most of the people who refused to go to Lebanon were not court-martialled. In most cases their units worked out some arrangement without it coming to trial. Those tried received sentences of about 28 to 35 days. However, some people got three or four consecutive sentences because once they got out of jail, they were again told to report to Lebanon, and they would take another sentence rather than go. I think our war-resisters group was unique in Israel at that time because we were willing to make a real sacrifice rather than simply holding up a protest sign on Saturday night and then going back to work on Sunday morning.

*   *   *

I was in Israel for almost 14 years before I got involved in peace issues. It was a gradual thing as I began to see things differently. For example, when I was a dorm counsellor at Hebrew University, I got to know some of the Arab students and visited their homes when I was on vacation. Then, at the end of the year, I found out that one of the students had been arrested for something I was quite sure was not his fault. I began to see how Arab students got into trouble for things that I, as an Israeli Jew, would never get into trouble for. I could be involved in leftist politics and nothing would happen to me, but immediately this Arab student got targeted. The double standard upset me, but I didn't choose to get further involved.

All of that changed in 1977 when Menachem Begin was elected prime minister. This was like a red light to me, and I was worried that with the Likud coming to power war might break out or the West Bank might be annexed. I felt I had to do something, and even though I was not very prominent in the formation of Peace Now, I was a member of the initial group. In 1978, I gave the first lecture about Peace Now in the United States at a conference of Jewish educators.

*   *   *

Ideologically I have been drawn together with many wonderful Jews and Arabs who are concerned about the rise of ideological discrimination of which Kahane is just the tip of the iceberg. The truth is that the rest of the iceberg goes much deeper and is more substantial than most Israelis are willing to admit.

There are levels that one goes through in contacts with Arabs. The first is polite — the hospitality and platitudes. Beyond that, dialogue can be very tricky and complicated. Arabs are suspicious of someone like me who is a religious Jew because their association with the religious community has been mostly negative. When they think of religious matters, these are things that close them out rather than build bridges.

And then a lot of Israeli Arabs wonder to what extent the state will ever fully recognize them as citizens. I think that makes them very cautious about dialogue. Why should they be involved in dialogue if in fact their status in society is a foregone conclusion? I think there was a time when Arabs were more interested in polite Jewish gestures towards them. Now there is a real suspicion that this is nothing but tokenism — something that will ease Jewish consciences.

* * *

The warmest reception I've had from Israeli Arabs was at Um-el-Fahm, the largest Arab village in Israel with a population of over 20,000 people. Israeli Jews see this town as a hotbed of Arab radicalism, and most of them wouldn't dream of going near it. I went there because of my involvement in interfaith dialogue. I was told to meet the mayor of Um-el-Fahm who had indicated an interest in coming to a conference I was trying to organize. I went to his home, and we became friends; he is a wonderful, warm person.

Some time later he called me and asked if I could come to Um-el-Fahm because Kahane was threatening to come there. Kahane wants all Arabs out of Israel, and for publicity's sake had decided to go to Um-el-Fahm to set up an "emigration office" so Arabs could sign up to leave the country.

I went to Um-el-Fahm and stayed in the mayor's house. Even though Kahane didn't show up, we had a great rally against his racist ideology. It was obvious, however, that everybody in that village was ready to strangle Kahane, and would have gladly lined up to take a shot at him. I was trying to say: "Look, we reject his ideology and everything he says, but we have to do it peacefully. We don't target the man, only his ideas."

A few weeks later Kahane did come to the village, and once again the mayor called me. I was worried that this time there might be violence because there wouldn't be the same kind of idyllic feeling we had at the the first rally.

When we drove up the next morning we found thousands of people sitting on the road chanting and singing. That went on for a few hours, and it was all non-violent. Then something happened: it was like a rumour swept through the crowd and stones started flying. The police, who were right opposite us, started with tear gas and everything deteriorated.

Kahane was not allowed into the village, but unfortunately the police were not telling the people that, and the lack of communication was creating suspicion and tension. At this point I saw people stockpiling weapons — not guns, but other kinds of dangerous stuff; the police were also bringing in extra forces. All of this made me sure that I was going to see somebody get killed before the day was out.

I went with a friend to the police lines and said: "Look, this is ridiculous. You are massing against them, and they are sure that you are going to charge into the village. Isn't there any way we can de-escalate this thing?"

I had never done anything like this before. I'd never tried to negotiate, but I had this sinking feeling that something awful was going to happen. The policeman said: "Well, tell them to stop throwing stones."

"They are throwing stones because they don't want you to come into the village," I said.

"But we aren't going into the village," he said. "Great," I said, "I'm going to tell them." After that things calmed down a bit.

Fifteen minutes later there were some more stones, and when tear gas started again I was somewhere between the police and the demonstrators. If I ran towards the police, I would be hit by the stones and would also be identified with the police, but if I ran back to the village, I'd be tear gassed. I chose to run towards the villagers, and as I ran I lost my kipa.

When the tear gas cleared there was still a face-off. I went back to look for the kipa, and since I was once again near the police line, I saw the same guy and said: "Look, we still have to try to de-escalate this thing because I'm very worried that somebody is going to get killed."

He told me to leave him alone. He was upset because his men were being hurt by the stones. Then this sergeant grabbed me and told me to get out. I didn't move fast enough so I was pulled through the ranks of troops, and was kicked and beaten. I couldn't believe what was happening. Here I was trying to make sure that things stayed peaceful, and ended up being beaten by police just because I was talking to someone.

When the whole thing was finally over, my friends who had seen me being beaten said that we had to find these policemen, identify them and complain. Finally we confronted the person, and I asked him if he had given an order to beat me. He said: "Yes, I gave the order, and I wish they had beaten you more." That wasn't true because I knew he hadn't given an order, it was just something that happened spontaneously. Eventually I was beaten again, charged with throwing stones at the police and was put in a stinking jail cell for eight hours. I wasn't hurt that bad physically — the other Arabs in the cell had been beaten worse than I — but my indignation was much greater than theirs. They were calm because, unlike me, they had never viewed a policeman as someone who wouldn't arrest them.

* * *

From that point on, a few things changed in my life. As a rabbi, I realized that I had to have a congregation. It wasn't enough to be an academic, I needed to have a congregation because I needed to communicate what I believed to people, people who would feel responsible to me and to whom I would be responsible. It was a relationship that I needed to create.

It also became clear to me that I could never condone the use of violence, not in the army and not in personal relationships. It was not just seeing how counterproductive the Um-el-Fahm violence had been, but it was also seeing how the police, who I imagine were decent people, lost their judgment in that violent situation. As a result I've tried to get non-violence more on the political left's agenda here in Israel. People in Peace Now, who have been heckled or beaten in demonstrations, have wished that they could hit back. It's a natural reaction, but I'm trying to get them to see that real strength comes when you realize that you are not going to hit back. Then you know you can take more, and then you know what you are there for. It's when you resort to violence that you lose your spiritual advantage.

There are all kinds of levels to work at and I'm not going to expect that everyone will be a pacifist. I believe in non-violence because I believe it is always better than violence. People's reactions to violence are infinitely worse than what happens in the violence itself.

* * *

I think there is something that most Jews in this country have not confronted. I know this puts me out on a limb, but I think we can't expect peace in this country without seriously questioning some of our presuppositions. What has been most painful for me is living daily with the fact that most Jews here would like this country to be a Jewish state, and are not aware of the fact that that is impossible.

It is impossible because you can't have a state which legitimizes something that only some of the people have. If you do, then someone like Kahane is an inevitability. What we are doing in Israel is making everyone other than Jews feel unwanted even if they constitute only 17 percent of the population. The Arabs in the state of Israel are told that this is a Jewish state, and all attempts to make that a law and build it into the structure only further their alienation.

Arabs can never really believe that they are involved in co-existence, and because of that they can never take Jewish humanism and morality seriously. As an Arab, it just doesn't register when you are being told that you don't belong, and when you call the state a Jewish state, you are telling Arabs that they don't belong.

I came to this country because I knew it was part of my Jewish destiny. I think that I can be a true Zionist and still maintain this faith though it must be a very carefully defined thing. This country doesn't have to be a Jewish state. Here Jews can achieve a quality of Jewish life that is impossible anywhere else because everywhere else we are a minority, and as such are always going to have to choose between maintaining our identity or assimilating.

Here in Israel we have another problem: by physically living here we Jews are supposed to guarantee our existence, but we are not guaranteeing our existence because we have become a country which is fighting for our rights against other people's rights. Here there is no concept of Jews working for all the citizens of Israel. We are working for the Jews, and the others are resented because, as some people say, they are getting a free ride. They don't have to go to the army or have other obligations so we resent them and, consequently, we are not working for them ideologically. There are lots of people who do work for the rights of Arab citizens so there is still something left of Jewish morality, but when it comes to the notion of this being an exclusively Jewish state, we are blindfolded because we cannot escape the consequences of excluding other people from the scene.

I think we have to reintroduce the distinction between state and religion in Israel. As a Conservative rabbi, I am ostracized and not recognized because the Orthodox have a monopoly. This pattern of having group interests which exclude other groups is, unfortunately, an all-pervasive pattern here. Judaism must be released from the grasp of nationalism. Right now it is in a vice, and what is being squeezed out are the most extreme forms of Judaism and nationalism intertwined. As a result a whole section of the Torah is being ignored.

We have to develop a sense of "Israeliness", meaning that whether you are a Jew or an Arab, you are an Israeli and you have rights. The Star of David and our national anthem — let's just say they are vestiges of how the state was created since it was created by Jews. Once we have grasped the reality that we are, in fact, a country of Jews and Arabs, we have to understand that the country is going to have to create a sense of Israeliness of which Jewishness is only a part. That means that the prime minister of Israel can't simply speak for the Jewish people any more, even though they might be his largest constituency.

* * *

Zionism means the communal reconstitution of the Jewish people in Zion, but it does not have to be at the expense of anybody else. We always claimed that the country had room for more people. Back when the British said there was no more room and they had to close the gates to immigration, we said no, there is room for development.

We are imprisoned by the burdens of our myths. We say the whole country will eventually become a place of refuge for the Jewish people, but there are ten million Jews abroad who are not coming. Let's say, God forbid, that something happens, and they all have to come here. Does that justify taking the land away from the Arabs in the villages in the Galilee? That is the myth at work — the notion that this country can only develop for Jews, and any kind of Arab development jeopardizes the destiny of the Jewish people because it makes the country less of a place of refuge.

We have to reach a situation where the Israeli Arabs will say: "Of course, we will let Jews come whenever they are in distress because we are partners here, and if we are partners with Jews, we will see Jews coming from abroad also as potential partners."

The Israeli Arabs are our allies, and we have to work on our partnership with them because they are our best ambassadors in the Middle East. We should want them to say: "Sure, it's great living in Israel. I don't mind living with Jewish neighbours, a Jewish prime minister and everything else. It's good for me economically, educationally, socially and even religiously."

They are our ambassadors, and the more we make them choose between being Palestinian or Israeli — when being an Israeli means forgetting about their pride and rights — the less we have a chance of being accepted in the Arab world. We need them and they need us.

* * *

I'm fighting for my kind of Zionism so that people who feel like I do can call themselves Zionists. We don't have enough people advocating a progressive type of Judaism, and the same is true for Zionism. A lot of my friends say: "What kind of a Zionist are you?" In the public's mind, Zionism is equated with settling the West Bank. To them Zionism means nationalism. Nationalism doesn't mean how the state is going to survive, but it means ultra-nationalism. It means people mix up the ends and the means. The land is not an end. The state is not an end.

Our survival doesn't have to be endangered by the Arabs living in Israel. We are both partners here. You know all the slogans: we are either going to learn to depend on each other, or we are going to hang side by side. This country has a notion that we are 3½ million Jews minus 700,000 Arabs so the net is 3 million, but the country is really 3½ million plus 700,000.

Hanna Marron

Hanna Marron, 62, is one of Israel's most well-known actresses who regularly appears on both the stage and television. Born in Germany, Marron began her acting career at the age of four. After immigrating to Palestine and finishing high school, she studied at the Habima Theatre's Drama School.

A victim of Middle East violence, Marron nonetheless is active in the Israeli peace movement, especially with the Peace Now group. Because of her own experience, she is particularly concerned that all parties in the Middle East conflict repudiate the use of terror tactics.

"My experience", she says, "only made me realize the futility of terror. Now my fight is against terror from either side."

I remember this young man... I was on my way to London for a film test, and there was an interval at Munich airport. This was in 1970 when there were not all these security measures. I was with the pilot who was a friend of mine, and we stayed a little longer in the transit area. We were walking out to the bus when there were some footsteps, and I turned around.

There was this young man whose eyes I remember. He had beautiful eyes, and then he said something I did not really understand. He said: "This is an attack and we are going to kill you."

This seemed to be completely impossible. How could this be happening to me? I think I went into some kind of shock because I began to think very slowly. The next thing I remember was the pilot on the floor struggling with this young man. Then there was shooting and running. Grenades were being thrown, and I stood there frozen like Lot's wife. I looked outside and saw that the bus was also being attacked, and thought that I had better get down on the floor.

I put my bag on my head and lay down. Then I got a very hard push in my leg, and thought that something must have happened to me. When I put my hand out, there was this very sticky stuff all around, and I remember thinking to myself: "So this is blood. It has such a nice colour." Then I lost consciousness because I was hit in the main artery on the back side of my knee.

I remember going under, and there was this blue haze all around me. For some strange reason, I began to struggle against this blue. Later the doctors told me that this is what happens when you lose your blood very quickly. I felt that this was a very bad blue even though it felt very nice. I came to again and lost consciousness several times, but every time I fought to wake up.

I was almost left there to die because a radiator had been hit, and there was steam everywhere. At the last moment somebody was running, and I heard them shout that there was a woman lying there so they came and saved me.

They had to cut off my leg. I had many operations, and stayed in Germany for three months. When I came home, I still had to undergo operations because my hip was also hurt, and I had all kinds of implantations. I'm apparently very tough because not much more than a year later, I was on the stage again. I was moving and standing, and now you see that I am fine. I work, walk, dance and do everything.

* * *

I was born in Berlin. Luckily, my father was very conscious of the situation from the beginning of Hitler. I remember people saying: "Jews like you, we like", but my father did not want to stay in Germany. At the time the British wanted people who had certain skills to come to Palestine, and since my father was an electrician, he got a certificate to come and work here.

We were not religious at all. As a matter of fact, when I was a child I did not even know what it meant to be Jewish. I was in a kind of special situation because from the age of four, I was a child actress. I performed in films, on radio and on the stage. In Germany I was known as "unser Hannerle" — our little Hanna. I guess you could say I was the German version of Shirley Temple.

My being Jewish was not really known. My father didn't look particularly Jewish, and both my mother and I were blond. We didn't have any traditional Jewish things in the house, but we did celebrate Chanuka. We also had a Christmas tree, and as a child I thought it was wonderful because I had two holidays and got a lot of presents.

On Easter we would look for eggs. I knew Passover was at the same time because we would go to the Seder. Like most children all I remember is having to sit around the table for a long time, and being very bored with that.

Before we left Germany things really began to change, even in the theatre. I remember that I was asked to read a poem for some well-known Nazi's birthday. My mother got very scared, and we went to tell him that I could not take the part. He asked why, and my mother told him we were Jewish. He got very white in the face and said: "Thank you, this could have cost me my head — a Jewish girl reading a poem at such an occasion."

I never got any explanation about anything. I just knew that my father wanted to come to Palestine, and I was very happy about the choice. My mother was unhappy, and she kept telling me it would be terrible because it was a place only of sand and camels.

As a child actress, I had been lonely and rather unhappy, but when I came to Palestine things changed completely, and I became a normal child. I'll never forget the excitement when we arrived at the port of Jaffa. We took a small Arab boat because the large ships couldn't come close enough to shore for us to disembark. As a nine year-old child, the colour and noise of Jaffa were lovely for me. After we arrived in Tel Aviv, I enrolled in school, and for the first time was able to go out in the street and play with children. For me this was absolute joy.

In Palestine I heard the word "Zionism" for the time and got very enthusiastic. For example, the Hebrew language was just beginning to be used, and I walked around with a little tag that said: "Jews, speak Hebrew." I would go into shops and tell the merchants to put up Hebrew signs.

* * *

I really did not have much contact with Arabs when I was young, though we did have some because there were many Arabs in Jaffa. We had an Arab woman who came to our house to do the laundry, and sometimes there would be Arab dancers in the street. We all loved it, and gave them money for dancing.

Later, of course, there was a lot of violence, and I suffered hearing about things happening during the different stages of the strife that erupted. After that there was a different approach, but I must confess that I never gave the Arab problem much thought. In my mind there was no such thing as a Palestinian people. There were Arabs who lived here — some were good and some were bad just as there were good and bad Jews. All I knew was that we Jews wanted to build a country, and I was here to be part of that effort.

There was sometimes danger and sad stories, but as far as I can remember I was much more concerned with aliyah, which meant getting Jews into Palestine at a time when the British wouldn't allow it. By that time the Holocaust had begun, and this was the problem that occupied me.

By the time I finished high school, I had to decide what to do with my life, and this occupied my whole time. As a matter of fact, I didn't want to be an actress, but there was no money and I had not been a good enough student to get a scholarship. In the end I decided to become an actress, and went to study at the drama school of the Habima Theatre which is now the national theatre of Israel.

* * *

When the Second World War broke out we Jews in Palestine didn't have to go to war, but we thought it was our moral duty to join the British army, and so I did. I served in the Women's Auxilliary Service and spent most of the time in upper Egypt.

I wanted to be a driver because I thought that would be a romantic thing to do, and saw myself with General Montgomery at El Alamein, etc! The British army, however, had a different idea, and they made me into a clerk which was terrible. I know I became the worst clerk ever in the British army.

After two years I was lucky because by that time there were a great number of volunteers from Palestine in the British army. The army decided that it was time to give some kind of culture and entertainment to the Jewish soldiers, so they gathered a performing troop, and I was called to be part of it. Thankfully, this saved me from the boredom of the typewriter. I spent the last two years of the war with this group, and we travelled all over Europe and Syria — wherever there were Jewish troops.

We began to get the full idea of what had happened in Germany when we started meeting survivors in the camps in Europe. It was different hearing or reading about the Holocaust, and then meeting it face to face. The problem of the survivors became dominant especially since the

British would not allow them into Palestine. We did our best to help some of the people, and would try to smuggle them in. Sometimes we did not succeed because the British police got them, but there were a few we managed to get in because we travelled by boat.

Still, there was no problem for me concerning the Arab world at all. I must say even now that when I think back, the whole geographical area around me did not exist. My life was concentrated on what was happening right here, right then.

* * *

After the war, I helped start a new theatre called the Cameri, which is now the municipal theatre in Tel Aviv. This took up all my time, and it was a real struggle. Sometimes there was not enough to eat, but they were wonderful years. I was never as happy as when I was hungry.

By that time the British were fighting the Irgun and the Haganah, and I was naturally more with the Haganah because they were all my friends. There was a cafe here in Tel Aviv where poets and actors would meet. It was also a centre of the Alyiah Bet — the illegal immigration that was trying to get shiploads of Holocaust survivors into Palestine.

Again the Arab question was something I was just not connected with. As I think about it now, it seems strange because there were attacks and murders. I must say I heard about the horrible thing that happened at Deir Yassin and I thought it was awful, but at the time it was not something I was really concerned about.

* * *

Finally, the dream came true: we had a country. I remember sitting at the radio listening to the UN Partition Declaration and, I cannot tell you, this was the most exciting thing that happened. But then the independence war started.

In spite of everything that has happened and what I now know, I cannot forget that we were attacked. Let's not forget it because Ben-Gurion was ready to make some kind of arrangement for the division of the country.

I don't have to tell you how difficult it was, how many of my friends died in this war. The Arabs had problems, but we also had problems. Don't forget that this was just after the Holocaust. Finally the real stories had come out, and we really went into shock. The Holocaust was there engulfing us, swallowing us up, and at the same time we were fighting for this little, tiny country while all these big countries around were trying to kill us. It was very difficult because no matter how humane we might be, no matter how much we cared for other people, we were fighting for our lives.

So there was the war and, heaven help us, we won, but Jerusalem was divided and we would go through the hills at night to give performances there. I remember times when we had to go in an armoured car from Tel Aviv to Petah Tikva because Arabs were sniping in Yarkon Street. A person right next to me was hit by a Jaffa sniper, so there really wasn't time to feel sorry.

* * *

Life went on. I was successful and became quite well known. Excuse me for saying this, but I became a bloody good actress. I was lucky too because I got wonderful parts. My personal life wasn't so happy because I was married and divorced twice, but my third marriage has lasted almost 28 years, and I have three wonderful children.

Now when you have children, things start to change, and you begin to think more about what is happening and especially about the future. When my son was born, I thought that by the time he became 18, there would be no more wars.

I am getting very emotional about this because through all the wars when friends were killed, I always asked why. Why couldn't we have peace? Why? This I know from all the people I have met as an actress — from Be'er Sheva in the south to Kiryat Shmona and Metulla in the north — we must have peace. People have different ideas on how to get it, but they want it so badly.

You must realize the frustration because terror crept in. Stereotypes were created and little children began to see in every Arab a terrorist. I fought against these feelings, but you know what it's like when you have a rapist who rapes three or four women? You begin to see a rapist in every man you meet. It takes great effort not to be captured by this thought, not to see the enemy in every Arab.

The stereotypes are not only on our side. When my husband and I visited Egypt, the people in the street were very friendly. A taxi driver looked at my husband and me and said: "You are Israelis. You are Jewish?"

"Yes, of course," I said. "My husband was even born in Israel."

He said: "Well, I don't understand. In school I learned that Israelis have two horns and a tail. Now I'm in shock because I meet many Israelis and I just don't understand."

My husband is an architect, and he wanted to meet Egyptian architects. I wanted to meet actors, but we just couldn't meet them. We were told that the intelligentsia are afraid because if they make contact with Israelis, they become outcasts.

This peace we have with Egypt is better than nothing, but it is a little, miserable peace. Israelis go by the hundreds to Egypt, but no Egyptians come here. If they would come, we could meet and have discussions. Maybe there would be some arguments, but at least the Egyptians would not be ghosts. We are afraid of ghosts. We want to speak to an enemy we can see, but also to an enemy who is willing to listen. I want to do everything I can to bring peace. There are more people than you think who are willing to do the same thing. True, there are those who are getting more and more belligerent and say, "Okay, enough", but don't forget that we have gone through many years of being afraid.

* * *

I've been invited with Peace Now to all kinds of meetings with Palestinians. Unfortunately, they have never been very successful. I am saying this quite candidly. We Israelis were all very eager to communicate, but we did not get one foot ahead. It was the Palestinians who would not budge one inch. We came to speak with them, and were ready to concede that the Palestinians have rights. We said we were ready to give back Gaza and the West Bank if we can live together, but they would not recognize our right to be here. In spite of the fact that I am still eager and willing to sacrifice anything I can to make peace, I must admit that this kind of attitude makes me boil.

I think that, as it is in most things, the leaders are actually responsible for what is going on, not the people. I am against all of this Israeli nationalism and what the religious people are trying to do with the West Bank settlements.

* * *

Terrorism has never solved anything in the world. Who suffers from it? The people, that's who. I don't know how it might be possible to get to the people in the Arab countries and find a way to talk so they can begin to understand that we are here to stay. I mean, I have planted trees in my garden, and I'm not going to move away. My children and my husband were born here. I want to stay and my children want to stay. I'm quite willing to share my life with those people who were here before, but please let me live in peace. Please let me not be frightened.

I have two beautiful daughters. They are very open, and they befriend young Arab people. I'm not against it because they are Arabs, but still I'm scared to death. I must say it. I am scared to death. I don't want to live this way.

It is difficult to explain or try to express, but even though I almost died and lost my leg, I don't hate Arabs. This experience only made me realize the futility of terror. Now my fight is against terror from either side. The fact that we now have people like Kahane or like those Jews who tried to attack the Arab buses — this is a terrible thing. I have friends who say: "Look what they did. They killed children." Okay, they did. It is awful and I hurt terribly because of it, but I believe that we Jews should not act the same way. We must be patient and we must find a way to talk to these people. It's not easy but we must do it.

The Palestinians must get rid of this terror machine, and look at the situation from another point of view. Look, we Jews are here to stay because we have already lost four or five million people elsewhere. It is impossible to throw us out because now most of us have been born here, and this is our homeland.

Of course we have to understand that the Palestinians were also born here. This is their country and they love it as we do, so let's find a way of meeting. It should be possible.

Daoud Kuttab

Daoud Kuttab is the 31 year-old editor of the weekly English edition of al-Fajr, the major Palestinian newspaper printed in the occupied West Bank. Kuttab's political commentaries have also been carried on the editorial pages of both The New York Times *and* The International Herald Tribune.

The son of a Protestant clergyman, Kuttab remembers his father teaching him two basic lessons: first, that he should not hate the Jews; and second, that he should be proud of his Palestinian heritage. "We Palestinians", he says, "are not interested in throwing Israelis into the ocean; we are only interested in what is ours, and for that we are willing to make compromises."

When the 1967 war began our family was separated. My father had been in Germany for some conference, and the morning of the war my mother was visiting in Jerusalem. My brother was in Bethlehem doing some shopping, and I was home alone with the children. I remember it was a Monday morning and we heard the siren, but during that time there had been a lot of training for air raids so the siren was kind of usual. I didn't take it to be anything serious. So I sat on the balcony, just watching. All of a sudden my brother came running and said: "What are you doing outside on the balcony? We have to go downstairs."

So we went down the basement, which was very dark and quiet, and we just sat in there not knowing what to do and listened to the radio. After a while we realized that many people who were in the suburbs of Bethlehem were going into the city. We lived on the outskirts of Bethlehem, near Rachel's Tomb, so we decided that we should go into the city where it might be safer and where my aunt had a big house.

We had no car, so we had to walk about two kilometers. My baby sister was less than a year old. The three year-old sister had stepped on a nail or something, so my elder brother Jonathan had to carry her and I carried the baby.

My aunt's house had been converted into a first-aid place. We put a big red cross outside, and since my mother is a nurse she tried to help people out. My cousin had a little Volkswagen, and he would drive around and pick up injured people and bring them to our house for first aid. Later they would be taken to a hospital.

During the second or third day of the war my aunt, who was the head nurse in the Beit Jala Hospital, came running from the hospital looking for my brother. She ran into the house and shouted: "Where is he? Where is he?" When she saw him, she just kissed him and went back, and we didn't know what the problem was. Later we found out that a corpse had come into the hospital — a headless corpse — and the body looked like my brother's, so she thought it was him, and she couldn't be convinced that it was not him until she saw for herself.

* * *

I remember the first days after the occupation began because a family near ours was caught by the Israelis — they suspected them of some kind of involvement — and they blew up their house. For my younger sister this was very traumatic because we knew the family, and to have your house blown up in 15 minutes was something that we children never forgot.

I don't remember what I thought of the war and the occupation because I was only 12 years old. The reality of it all didn't dawn on me. I realized after the war that there were differences because a friend of ours had died, but the whole implication of occupation didn't become real to me until much later in life.

There were changes though. During the summers we used to go and spend time with my uncle who lived in the Jordan Valley on the East Bank. We looked forward to that very much, but after the war we knew that we could not go there any more.

During the war my father had been trapped outside the country so he went to Amman to try, through the Red Cross, to come back to us. The Israelis told the Red Cross that he could come back, and when he tried to come back they wouldn't allow him. He went back to Amman and again they promised that he could come. Two or three times he tried to come back, but he was not allowed to return. Finally, my uncle smuggled him across the border at the north part of the Jordan River. People were wading across the river. They would wait for the Israeli jeep to go by and then they would cross. It was very dangerous.

* * *

I knew almost nothing about Israelis before the war. There were, however, some Israelis living at the Hebrew University on Mt Scopus, and every Wednesday a convoy would take food to them there. I went to a school in Jerusalem called St George's School, and every Wednesday at about 10 o'clock the students would stand on the edge of the school playground and look over and watch these armour-clad convoys go by. Sometimes we would throw stones at them.

I also had a schoolmate who lived up Nablus Road. His house overlooked "No Man's Land", so we used to go into the backyard and look over across the street and see the Israelis moving around. It was always a strange thing to see them through binoculars.

Before 1967, we really did not discuss the Israelis. It just was not a topic of conversation in our house and I don't think it was in other homes either. My parents were too busy with their lives and raising a family. The Israelis just weren't part of our lives — just like if you live in Jordan now, you don't discuss the Israelis unless you have relatives in the West Bank who talk about them.

After 1967, I had no personal relationships with Israelis. Some would come as tourists to Rachel's Tomb, and since we children had nothing to do, we started making lemonade and sold it to them. Beyond selling lemonade, I never got to know any Israeli personally. They were only soldiers standing at a checkpoint or they were the tourists. I don't remember ever being frightened of them. When I heard of people being killed I was upset, but I was never frightened of soldiers.

* * *

When I was 14 my parents moved to the United States. We went there because my parents wanted us to get a higher education, and at that time we had very few possibilities in the West Bank. Later I studied at Messiah College in Pennsylvania where I majored in business administration. I came back here when I was 24 because I was offered the job of business manager of this newspaper. When we got the licence for the English version of the paper, I moved over to this edition.

I had problems in the United States because I was struggling to find my own identity. I was in American society where everybody was supposed to assimilate into the melting pot and I was fighting against that. I would be an American during the day and an Arab at night at home. There was this kind of split personality and I really suffered from that. I think that the moment I returned here, it was as if there had never been a problem, and I felt that this was where I should have been.

The way my father brought us up had a profound effect on all of us children. He preached to us, and we really believed the idea that one should not hate one's enemy. The whole idea of loving your enemies was engraved on us from our childhood.

My parents were not ashamed of our Palestinian heritage or our identity. My father always talked about where he came from and where he grew up, so this subject was kept alive in our memories. Even when we were in America, my father continued to teach us Arabic because he did not want us to forget our language.

There are two main things my parents taught me that have left a lasting impression: the first is that I should not hate the Jews as a people. I didn't have to be happy with what they did, but as people I should not hate them. And second, I should be proud of my heritage, of my language, and the history of my people. On that there should be no compromise.

I really don't hate. First, I am very careful to differentiate between Jews and Zionists even though they are one and the same here in Israel. But I don't have anything against the Israelis and Zionists that I know. I don't hate them in the sense that I want to see them dead. Sometimes I feel sorrow more than hate, because I feel that they are leading their own nation into a very dangerous situation.

When I see human rights violations taking place, I try to remedy this through my work. It is a relief for me to inform people about what is happening, and it's a way for me not to hate. I think a lot of hate happens when you see something that is bad and you can't do anything about it, so you just start boiling. I feel that when I am doing something about what I have seen and what I know, I no longer have the time to hate.

* * *

The majority of Israelis that I know are people I have met in the course of my work as a journalist. You know, our life here really does not involve Israelis because the shopkeepers are not Israelis, and for the most part we don't have to go out of our own community to buy things.

My usual relationships are either with journalists or perhaps those Israelis who are involved in the theatre. I don't have Israeli friends who are the kind you would spend the weekend with. We have had lunch and have planned to invite each other to our homes, but so far that has not happened.

Most of the Israeli journalists I know understand me. During some of our discussions they clearly show that they know the kinds of things that serve the cause of the Palestinians. They are aware of what our goals are, and I think most of them are sympathetic towards our cause in one way or another. They understand and they try to show this in what they write, even though some of their editors are not interested in it. You can feel an understanding and an interest on their part to cooperate. Maybe to an extent our relationships are based on that, and the more they can understand our cause, the better our relationships become.

* * *

I would like people to know that we Palestinians genuinely seek peace. I would like them to understand that we are not interested in throwing Israelis into the ocean; we are only interested in having what is ours, and even for that we are willing to make compromises. We are a kind, generous people — we are not evil. We are not monsters with horns. We are just like any other people in the world, and like everybody else we have the bad and the good. But in general, we are a people who are seeking a just and honourable peace.

Practically, I think there are two levels of peace-making here. One I would call the national/political level and one I would call the human rights level. On the human rights level, I would like to see the violations stopped, and I would like to see the local people given a serious opportunity to express themselves politically — whether in municipal elections, a national referendum, or just in deciding how their taxes should be spent.

Nationally, I want an Israeli declaration recognizing that we Palestinians are a people, that we have rights, and that we have a right to determine our future. Ultimately, I hope that the Israelis will withdraw from the occupied territories and begin negotiations with our representatives. I would expect the international community to recognize the group that we have chosen as our representatives, just as we realize that to negotiate with Israel we have to recognize the Knesset and the Israeli government as their representatives. We only want the same, reciprocal recognition.

I would also like Israel and the international community to let us know what we can hope for. The international community should ask Israel what it plans to do with us — the Palestinians. Are they going to give us freedom or not? Are they going to give us a state or not?

* * *

There is no doubt that Israelis have a lot of fear. The problem is that I am not sure we are to blame for it. I mean we were not responsible for the Holocaust, but I understand that the idea of "never again" is very strong in the Jewish mind. They never again want to be in the kind of situation that happened in the Holocaust. But we also have fears. We don't want Sabra and Shatilla to happen again. We don't want what has happened, and what is happening now, to continue. We are, I think, in a much more immediately frightening situation.

If there is a particular fear that all Palestinians have, it is the fear of physical expulsion from this place. Ultimately, though, I think that time is on our side. The demographics of the situation certainly are on our side. Especially if Israel annexes the West Bank, the only way for Jews to remain in the majority would be for them to physically expel the Palestinians. So if there is one single fear that we have, it is the fear of physical expulsion.

Meir Kahane really doesn't bother me so much because I don't see in him anything that is so new and unique. I feel that deep down, most of the Israeli leaders have similar internal views and Kahane is just the public expression of their views. I'm more worried about somebody like the former Israeli Army Chief of Staff, Rafael Eitan, who is in a very powerful position and who has similar racist ideas. He is much more dangerous and more powerful. I should be very worried about Ariel Sharon because he is a person who has just as racist an ideology as Kahane, and is at the ministerial level in government and wields a lot of power.

* * *

How can I help the Israelis get rid of their fears? It is simple: security result from having secure borders and an internal security apparatus. No matter how far your borders are placed, you may always have an enemy on the other side of the border. If you take over all of Lebanon, you are going to have somebody on the other side of that new border. If you occupy Jordan, you will have somebody on the other side. No matter how far you expand, you will always have someone on the other side. So, in addition to making military preparations, one must make peace with one's neighbours. This is the best security. I mean you can be well equipped, so that when your enemy fires you can fire back, but there is no way you can stop him from firing the first shot unless you can have peace with him. Peace is the best military defence you can have.

The second thing is this: if the Israelis would allow a Palestinian state to be established, this new state would be the best guarantee for Israel's safety. How? It would mean that after 38 years of struggling, and after sacrifices and after bloodshed, we Palestinians would have the thing that we have been yearning for. As the leaders of the Palestinian state, we would see to it that we do not lose this thing that we have been dreaming about. We would make sure that nobody would fire a gun at Israel because we know that if this would happen, the very powerful Israeli army would take over the West Bank in 24 hours.

Beginning in 1981, Israel's northern border was quiet for 11 months. The PLO was involved in a ceasefire and it kept the guns quiet. So, when we are involved, we are the best group to protect Israel because we will not be doing it for Israel's sake, we will be doing it for our own sake. Having peace with your neighbours and giving the Palestinians what they want not only removes the reason for hostility, it also includes a new element of Arab protection for Israel.

I am worried that this whole thing will just take too long, that a solution will not be found in my lifetime, that it will take a couple of generations before there is a settlement. I'm afraid that the solution will come only after more bloodshed. Every new settlement that is built puts an additional obstacle in the way of finding a solution, and the Israeli settlers have no idea of ever withdrawing. This is the problem. This is going to make finding a solution more difficult, probably more tragic, and it will take longer and both sides will have to suffer more.

* * *

I see my contribution to the situation like this: We have a major information gap. Whether it is the Israelis or the international community, both really don't know what is going on here in the West Bank. When I tell them things, they always say: "Oh, we didn't know it was like that. We never heard that in our press."

The second thing I do is try to suggest the practical things that can be done to improve the situation. For example, I was in the United States a month ago, and I told people there why it is important that we have municipal elections here. Everywhere I went I said: "Listen, this is not a national thing; it's not a threat to Israel; it's only something to help the Palestinians run their own municipal affairs."

I feel that I also have a role to play in trying to improve our people's psyche — our people's emotions. We have to provide hope for our people and help them reconcile themselves to the situation they are in. We must try to help them stay in this country. We should try to help them build institutions that will give them hope and a feeling of confidence in themselves. If I can help give them that, then I feel that I am also helping them stand on their own two feet. Until the Palestinian people can stand on their own feet, it is going to be very difficult for any negotiations to happen.

We are economically dependent on Israel. We are politically dependent on the Arab and the international communities. I feel that we need to draw ourselves away from the negatives outside and try to build a positive element in ourselves, whether it is economic or political independence. We need to be able to say what we want, not have others say it for us. We need to establish the norms and the kind of way of life that we want — rather than what somebody might establish for us. By doing that we would be strong enough, our will would be strong and the fabric of our society would be strong enough, to make peace as well as the compromises that are necessary for peace.

At the present time, we feel defeated. We have accepted the fact that we have been defeated. Standing on our own two feet would help us refuse the defeat and work to change the situation. Some people say that this situation we are in is all God's will, that we shouldn't do anything about it, only go about doing what we can to survive in this mess. Standing on our own feet would mean realizing what kind of situation we are in, and that we can control our destiny if only we take it into our own hands. We have to work to change the situation; it will not change by itself. It won't change by any forces from the outside because the change has to come from within us.

* * *

I'm interested in helping provide avenues and the infrastructure for hope. A few years ago we didn't have a Palestinian theatre in Jerusalem.

Today we have a nice theatre, and the fact that it is here and people can go and see a play is something that gives people hope. They say: "Okay, we can do something. There is something creative within us." It gives them hope because they realize that they have something to offer; they have the ability to participate in creative things.

We need to work on providing jobs so we can develop our economy and our industry. When a person graduates and comes to ask for a job, if I can offer one, that's hope. A person doesn't need nice words, but needs to know that at the end of the month there will be a salary check. It's good to have this feeling that you are not alone in the community, that there are people who are supporting you. These are some ways to give people hope.

* * *

I don't have specific dreams; I have general dreams. I dream of being able to drive to Nazareth and continue on to Beirut. I would like to go and see my uncle's family in Amman without it being a historical experience that I wait months to prepare for.

I would like to get up in the morning and participate, maybe only in a small way, in the decisions that our leaders are making. It would be nice, when I complain about the holes in my street, to have the person at the municipality speak to me on the phone in Arabic, not Hebrew. I would like to go myself to the city hall and find out who is responsible for the holes in the street and the lights not working.

I want to be involved, and I want to know that we have a choice, a role in our future. The Israelis make choices. I would like to be able to vote in elections every now and then. I would like to be involved in criticizing the new Palestinian state if it is not doing something about women's rights, or when the workers are being unfairly treated, and so on. I don't want to spend the rest of my life complaining about the Israelis. That is not my future.

I want to be involved in building my own future rather than trying to destroy Israel's future in the hope that somehow that will help me build mine. After all this destruction, we would have to begin all over again, and I don't want to begin again. I just don't want to be involved in any destruction.

I would be happy if the Israelis would withdraw peacefully, but unfortunately I see this happening only if they are pressured to do so. If there is another war, then directly or indirectly I'm involved in this cycle of destruction. I don't want this to happen. I want to be involved in building rather than destroying.

Yehezkel Landau

Yehezkel Landau is the 37 year-old information director of Oz veShalom (strength and peace), a religious, Zionist peace movement in Israel. The organization's name comes from Psalm 29:11: "The Lord will grant his people strength, the Lord will bless his people with peace."

The religious Jews who founded Oz veShalom felt it was necessary to clarify the order of religious priorities amid what Landau calls "the messianic rhetoric that was polluting the atmosphere and blinding people to some of the deeper Judaic values that, among other things, teach us to honour humanity by recognizing the sacred image of God in our enemy, even if he is fighting us".

Landau is a graduate of Harvard University and Harvard Divinity School where he studied psychology, religion and education. In addition to his work with Oz veShalom, he lectures on Judaism and interfaith relations at Nes Ammim, the Christian communal village in western Galilee. He also teaches at St George's College and in the international study programme of the Sisters of Sion, both in Jerusalem.

What I try to tell Palestinians is that we Israelis are afraid of them. This is very hard for them to understand and believe. How can we be afraid of them? They have far fewer weapons, if any, and we are supposed to be this great military power. But it has nothing to do with guns and uniforms; it is all in the soul.

It's like Jacob, in Genesis 32, coming home and fearing that Esau will take revenge on him for something that happened twenty years before: the way he got the birthright and the blessing in not quite a "kosher" way. Plus you must remember that the PLO has used terror tactics against innocent civilians, including women and children. It's not only the actual terror, it's the verbal violence — the rhetoric — as well. This physical and verbal violence has only fed the traumatic constellation of feelings that the Jews have in this country. If I could say one thing to the Palestinians, it would be: "On your side do what you can to defuse this trauma because it is the biggest obstacle in the way of a Palestinian state." The Palestinians and Israelis have two national mythologies that discount and delegitimize the experiences of the other. It all starts in the gut by rationalizing one's pain, suffering and grief. If you suffer you want to pin it on somebody else. It is very interesting to see how the word "Nazi" gets thrown around here: the Israelis act like Nazis; the Palestinians act like Nazis; the PLO acts like Hitler. Soon the devil incarnate is represented in your enemy, and that means that you do not have to honour his experience. The enemy becomes dehumanized and demonized.

Since we Jews are still so close to Hitler and evil on such a mass scale, the tendency is to project that recent memory on to the present conflict, and thereby mystify it. The situation becomes an all-or-nothing, black or white, Manichaean holy war. Compromise is impossible because the enemy is like the enemy of God, and how can you compromise with the enemy of God? You can't. You can only keep fighting, believing that God is on your side and will help you win.

This kind of behaviour makes it difficult to know what the other side is feeling because you don't want to communicate, you only want to win. Thomas Merton wrote an essay called "War and the Crisis of Language". In our world, he said, we use weapons as a means of communication because we don't want to find the right words. Weapons fill the vacuum in communication; they take over where words leave off and communicate a very clear, unambiguous message. Both sides to a protracted conflict come to prefer the deadly "dialogue of the deaf" rather than risk listening to the appeal of the "enemy".

* * *

I was born in Santiago de Chile because my father's job took him to South America after the Second World War. My parents grew up between the wars in Vienna, and independently fled Austria in 1938. My mother went to Panama where she had an uncle, and my father went to New York. They met and eventually were married in New York. After the war, an American army buddy of my father's got him a job with MGM films as their South American representative, and that is how he ended up in Santiago. When I was 3½ years old we moved to the United States.

I grew up in suburban America in a middle class, ethnically mixed New York community. We had a sizeable Jewish community, but it was by no means homogeneous so I had a pluralistic upbringing. That experience has, I'm sure, made me very sensitive to what I find here in Israel: a polarized society where people live and go to school separately because cultural integration is not really seen as an ideal.

Clearly, from my home and school environment and also from the religious school I attended, I was able easily to mix Judaism and pluralism, and I never had a problem balancing the particular and the universal. If I had grown up in Israel, I probably would have had more of a struggle trying to balance these two dimensions of Jewish spirituality because separation of religion and state does not work in this country. It doesn't work because this is the "Holy Land". This situation is true not only of the Jewish community but of the Palestinian as well.

* * *

I first came to Israel in April 1978, and it's interesting that I was the last person in my family to come and the only one who stayed. I did my undergraduate degree at Harvard University in psychology, religion and education, and returned to the Divinity School for my second degree which is in the same field. My background was in Reform Judaism, and in the course of my studies, I became more Jewishly observant and began to define myself more as a religious educator coming from a traditional Jewish base.

After teaching for a couple of years at a small, liberal arts college in upstate New York, I came here. In the United States I had seen how the image of what was happening in this land came filtered across the television screen, and how it was reported in the newspapers. Some of these were very violent, ugly images, and I felt a lot of anguish about what was happening here. By being at a distance from it, I felt as though I was looking through a glass darkly. At least if it was not dark, it was blurry, and I wanted to see this land from the inside looking out.

Because I was born in 1949, Israel has always been here for me, though I never took it for granted. I appreciate what the world was like for Jewish people before Israel was created. The recreation of a Jewish commonwealth in the land of Israel ushered in a revolutionary way of thinking for Jews, and I came here to see what that would mean for me, both personally and professionally.

I also came to study in Jerusalem, and spent my first two years studying in an Orthodox yeshiva. Through daily prayer and other observances, I deepened my Jewish knowledge and commitment. Considering my studies in theology and psychology, I thought that Israel would not only be a living laboratory, but also a field of vocational service for me. I didn't know where I would find my niche professionally, but I felt the holiness of this place calling me. There was also a need for people to work for peace and reconciliation, and this was very much in my mind when I came here.

By the time I met Dalia, my wife, and had got married, things were rather solidified. I was quite well prepared for this place. I was not surprised, and I certainly have not been disillusioned. I didn't expect to find any kind of rose garden or utopia here.

* * *

My first experiences with Palestinians came through my two-year job with the Israel Interfaith Association. I was coordinating various educational programmes, and in that capacity was meeting with Arabs who are citizens of the state of Israel. My contact with Palestinians from the occupied territories or Jerusalem was infrequent, but I made it my business to try to meet them, and I suppose the main reason I left that job and created my present position was the desire to be more actively involved in the political dimension of inter-religious work. I wanted to address the conflict from my own religious perspective and not just speak in academic terms about the past or theological subjects like the Jewishness of Jesus. Granted, these subjects are very interesting, but if they don't have something to do with the existential reality of people's lives — where they live, where they hurt, how they deal with the conflict and try to make justice and peace a real thing here — I get frustrated.

I also felt it was absolutely incumbent upon observant Jews, who were portrayed in the media as fanatic extremists, to work for social healing. I still feel this way and it is one of the most important reasons for doing this work. I want to combat the desecration of God's name by people who should know better, and who in the name of God do unjust or evil things. Whether they are Jews, Christians or Muslims, I think this is the thing that God must be most unhappy about.

* * *

I can't say I have been surprised about my relationships with Palestinians because I had no preconceived notions about them. I have tried to be empathetic and sympathetic, and I assume that I would share their views if I were in their shoes. I try to understand the twentieth-century experience in this land from their point of view. Of course I have read quite a bit to try to put their individual views into historical perspective, and I've come to understand that the two peoples have different, subjective interpretations about what this conflict is all about.

The Jewish people's experience is one of "coming home". This means that at last we are compensated for 2000 years of anti-Semitism which culminated in the Holocaust. However, the Palestinians say that we shouldn't have a Jewish state at their expense. To them Zionism means that we have occupied and taken over at least a part of their country, if not the whole thing. Their being on the receiving end of Zionism is perceived as some kind of a colonial invasion, and I can understand why they see it that way especially since the first waves of Jewish immigrants came from Europe. They came on the coat-tails of Lord Balfour and the British Empire so it is not surprising that the Palestinians should see the Jews as Western European or American agents and aliens.

What we perceived was the rebuilding of our mother country which had been dismembered 2000 years ago. We weren't a colony of some other mother country; this *was* the mother country, and this is what the Palestinians have such a hard time understanding: that the Jews have at least an equal right to an independent commonwealth in the Holy Land. This means Jews should have self-determination as a people, not as individuals, and it is a tough thing — the toughest thing — for Palestinians to accept.

For me, Judaism is not just an affair of the synagogue and the kosher kitchen; it is supposed to be the agenda of a whole society in this land. That is what the Bible says we are supposed to be, and the condition of exile, diaspora, and minority status is not the normative, desirable status for Jews. History has taught us that it is also dangerous.

The religious underpinning of our homecoming, even if most of the people who now live here are not outwardly pious, practising Jews, is difficult for Palestinians to see because the outward manifestations of it are either secular, or maybe fanatically religious. To put a positive, religious interpretation on Zionism is virtually impossible for most Palestinians. This I accept. It is part of my job to try to present an alternative to both the secular, humanistic interpretation of Zionism and

Gush Emunim's pseudo-messianic interpretation. That is why I want my work to offer an alternative to those two extremes.

* * *

I suppose I don't feel fully understood, especially in spiritual terms, even by my closest Palestinian friends, but I don't necessarily think I have to be fully understood to be accepted here. The fact is that since we have more military and economic power at the moment, we can afford to broaden our horizons and try to understand the other side in positive terms. Maybe we can even reach the point of understanding that if we were Palestinians, we would also be nationalistic and resisting Zionism — certainly the pseudo-messianic Zionism in secular terms of an Ariel Sharon, or in religious terms of a Rabbi Levinger.

I have never yet heard a Palestinian tell me that if he were a Jew he'd be a Zionist. Once a Palestinian friend from the West Bank happened to come through Yad Vashem, the Holocaust memorial museum in Jerusalem, with a group of us who were participating in an international interfaith conference. Afterwards he said: "I now understand why you are so obsessed with security. It never dawned on me that the Nazi period was so evil and cruel, and that you had suffered so much."

Until the great majority of Palestinians go through Yad Vashem, I don't expect that they will understand me or the majority of the Jewish people who are living just one generation after the Holocaust. They just won't be able to see that for us Zionism is a matter of life or death, just as a Palestinian state with its own Law of Return is a matter of life or death for them.

As we are talking here, there is another Shiite bombardment of the Sabra and Shatilla refugee camps in Beirut, and Arafat is saying that there has to be an Arab liberation force to protect Palestinian lives. The cruel tragedy is that it is other Arabs, not Israelis, who are at this moment threatening their lives.

After the Sabra and Shatilla massacre in the fall of 1982, I tried to get an article published in which I argued that the Israeli government should offer to resettle, in the West Bank, Palestinian refugees who were under our military jurisdiction in south Lebanon. There were something like 60 to 80,000 Palestinian refugees in the area from Beirut down to the southern border, and after Sabra and Shatilla they were living in fear of another Phalangist massacre. They feared that they were the next candidates for genocide and the world wouldn't care.

I made this suggestion, in part, to take moral and political responsibility for what had happened in Sabra and Shatilla, even though Israel was not directly responsible for the massacre. I also hoped we would do it in order to let the Palestinians know that we were interested in their survival, and that we could be the key to their liberation and homecoming. If they were really willing to make peace with us, we could help them come home and create a state in the West Bank and Gaza. I thought the best way to prove this would be to say, before negotiations about whose flag flies where, that we Israelis want them to live side by side with us. Simple... right? Well, the article didn't get published. The few Knesset members I circulated it to didn't do a thing. The idea was just too radical, the idea of wanting your enemy to live.

* * *

Oz veShalom was started in 1975 by a group of religious kibbutz leaders, academic people and some politicians in the National Religious Party who felt that Gush Emunim had distorted the traditional, moderate message of religious Zionism, and virtually hijacked the National Religious Party to serve its goal of settling the occupied territories. We felt this kind of activity was leading Israel down a very dangerous road, and we were also against any mystification of the conflict that might lead people to believe that God has to bless us and help us no matter what we do, as long as we are faithful to a certain vision of what the land of Israel should be.

We support a willingness, painful as it may be, to sacrifice Israeli control over parts of this Holy Land. There are places in the West Bank like Hebron and Shechem-Nablus which are holy to us. We hesitate to give them up because from 1948 to 1967 Jews could not go to the Western Wall in Jerusalem, or to the Tomb of the Patriarchs in Hebron. In 1967 these places were conquered in a defensive war, and to give them up again to Arab sovereignty is a painful sacrifice which can only be justified in the name of something higher than whose flag flies above them. That something higher is: saving life, making peace, and bringing justice to both peoples so each has sovereignty over part of the land.

Oz veShalom felt it was necessary to clarify the order of religious priorities amid messianic rhetoric that was polluting the atmosphere and blinding people to some of the deeper Judaic values. For example, religiously humanistic values that teach us to honour humanity by recognizing the sacred image of God in our enemy, even if he is fighting us. To do that we have to try to understand why he is fighting us, and discover ways to resolve the conflict.

Now if you are fighting somebody like Hitler, your enemy has forfeited the image of God, and you can only fight and defeat him. But if you are fighting Palestinian nationalism over control of God's holy land, it's not the same kind of conflict, and that is what people here don't understand.

* * *

To the Palestinians Oz veShalom tries to say that Judaism and Zionism are not negatives. Zionism is not just a secular political reality, whereas Judaism is considered to be a blessed spiritual heritage from Moses. Zionism is based on Judaism and you can't divorce the two. We are religious Zionists because we are faithful Jews, and that means that for us the biblical word "Zion" has a religious *and* a political meaning.

It means that we have a right, alongside the Palestinians, to a Jewish state here — a Jewish state, not a Jewish ghetto. That state does not bar Palestinians from living here, but nevertheless it must be a state defined in Jewish terms, with a Jewish majority and a mostly Jewish government. This Jewish state should exist alongside an Arab state called Falastin (Palestine), perhaps confederated together with Jordan, as are the Benelux nations.

Our message to Israeli Arabs is that they should have full civil rights as a minority in a Jewish state comparable to what I would enjoy in the United States as a minority within a majority, non-Jewish culture. They should have a choice. Maybe they will want to be dual citizens of Israel and Palestine: I have retained my American citizenship, but I consider myself an Israeli first. They could choose to be a minority in a Jewish state, or be part of the majority in a Palestinian state.

* * *

Christianity, especially in Europe, expressed its identity as somehow being incompatible with even a Jewish minority in its midst, and every now and then tried to get rid of it. This anti-Jewish undercurrent has been part of Christian history for the last 2000 years. Therefore, I find myself somewhere between annoyance and anger when Christians use double standards in judging Israel. We are supposed to live up to some saintly ideal, or else we forfeit our right to exist as a separate state here. That is not a fair judgment, especially since we have been at war since the day

this state was created. Yes, I know, that is part of the Christian legacy —
the negative part.

The positive part is that the gospel really could inspire Christians to
play a reconciling role by trying to identify with both sides, seeing the
justice in each claim and trying to create an atmosphere for compromise.

It seems to me that the official statements that come out of the World
Council of Churches or the National Council of Churches of Christ in the
USA don't come to grips with the potential that the world Christian
community has to help bring Israeli Jews and Palestinian Arabs closer
together. The statements usually sound like this: Israel has a right to exist;
the Palestinians have a right to self-determination and their own state; the
PLO is the legitimate representative of the Palestinians so Israel has to
talk to the PLO.

Now, by just looking at the last ten years during which these statements
have been part of the international scene, I don't think they have helped
very much. One of the reasons may be that there is nothing biblical,
nothing Christian or theological, in such statements. A political observer
anywhere could make these statements. I've asked church leaders in
Europe and the United States why they don't speak some biblical
language about this particular conflict. It would help the Palestinians
understand the biblical basis of Zionism and help Jews, especially in
Israel, understand our biblical roots in the Book of Genesis where all of us
not only got our start, but where the beginnings of the monotheistic
presence are felt.

What I hear when I talk with Western and Palestinian Christians is a
strong affinity with the liberation theology that comes out of Latin
America and South Africa. When this model, based on the Book of
Exodus, is imposed on this conflict situation, I think it is misleading and
wrong. I don't think that what we have here is simply one oppressed
people fighting an oppressor people. It's two oppressed peoples fighting
over the same holy land, and just because one has more weapons than the
other does not mean that it is any less oppressed. Certainly it has been no
less oppressed in the immediate past.

The Book of Genesis is the basis of my liberation theology for this
situation because I think the motif that runs throughout the book, from
Cain and Abel to Joseph and his brothers fighting for the birthright and
God's blessing, is really what this conflict is all about. Since Jews and
Muslims constitute the majority of the people fighting here, it would be a
wonderful, biblical contribution to reconciliation if Christians could
understand that the sons and daughters of Isaac and Ishmael are now

fighting over the Abrahamic blessing, and that somehow they have to share the blessing.

* * *

I'm hopeful but not optimistic. In the ultimate sense I'm hopeful, but in the short term I don't assume people will be able to overcome all the psychological baggage that keeps them stuck where they are.

My hope is based on the Book of Genesis so I try to put the present situation within the perspective of our 3000 years of ups and downs. In my lifetime I may not see any great "ups", although the Sadat visit was a real foundation for hope because it proved that both Jews and Arabs can turn around and be transformed — can experience metanoia in the New Testament sense, or *teshuvah* in Jewish terms.

I can't count on direct divine intervention to save us from our follies, but I still place my faith in the human capacity for transformation, which is given to us by the grace of God. That's the basis of my hope. Now, whether or not that transformation will happen fast enough, I don't know. It all depends on the courage of a few and the wisdom, or good sense, of a great many people.

Jean Zaru

Jean Zaru, 46, lives in the West Bank town of Ramallah. A Quaker by birth, Zaru has taught ethics and Christianity at the Friends Boys' School in Ramallah, and has been involved in the local and international YWCA for many years. She has also been active in the World Council of Churches, and has participated as a panel member in a number of international WCC gatherings.

Zaru believes that the Palestinian struggle for self-determination will only be successful through non-violent means.

She is a committed peace-maker who feels the message of non-violence is especially important at a time when many are discouraged about peace prospects in the Middle East. "We do not fight violently," she says, "because our ultimate goal is a better society for everyone. We want to get rid of evil, not people."

My family's living in Ramallah goes back to my great, great grandparents. Ramallah has traditionally been a Christian town, and was founded by our ancestors at the same time Columbus was exploring the shores of America. I have spent most of my life there, and have always enjoyed the sense of community that we have. People of many faiths live together without any problems or misunderstandings. Today there are Anglicans, Quakers, Lutherans, Roman Catholics, Greek Catholics, Orthodox, two groups of Baptists and other fundamentalist groups in Ramallah. My immediate family is not large. I have three sisters and one brother, but because my mother and father are first cousins the rest of the family is very large. Now many of my relatives live in the United States because of the wars and the lack of possibilities for work and education here.

My father had a coffee house in Ramallah, and it was the place where people could meet and share their views. He did not make a lot of money, but the coffee house was known as the place where doctors, engineers, teachers and others could meet and discuss things.

My parents were married under the care of the Ramallah Quaker Meeting because, as first cousins, they were not allowed to marry in the Orthodox Church. The customs of our culture do not forbid this marriage, but unfortunately many cousins who were Orthodox and wanted to marry had to seek out other churches. My mother chose the Quaker Meeting because she had graduated from the Friends Girls' School.

* * *

I was only eight years old in 1948, but I vividly remember that time. My father had many friends and relatives from both Lydda and Ramle. When the war started these people sought refuge by moving east, and they really suffered because they had to walk long distances in the heat of the summer. My father took my 12 year-old brother, and they went with trucks of bread and water to offer to these people who had been walking in the heat. Many of them were at the point of collapse because they had no food or water.

About one hundred of these refugees came and lived out of doors in our garden, and one family shared our three-room apartment. We were ten people in that apartment for about a year until they found another place. The Quaker Meeting House also provided shelter for many of them until we found other places. I especially remember the anguish of the women when they spoke about how some of them couldn't carry their children, and the babies were dying because they had no water. All of them carried the keys to their homes thinking that the danger would pass and eventually they would go back home. Most of the women had put on two dresses, and had buried their valuables in their houses.

The women, it seemed, suffered the most. They had such a hard life trying to raise their children out of doors. There was no running water, and the children would always be fighting because there was nothing else for them to do.

My brother was also influenced by the refugee situation and as a result he committed himself to promoting the cause of justice. After he graduated from Haverford College as a chemical engineer, he went on to take another degree from Harvard University in political science and Middle Eastern studies. For the last ten years he has been among the disappeared in Lebanon. We don't know exactly what happened to him, but I think he was caught in the midst of violence. Which party took him, or eliminated him, or has him in jail, we don't know, but we have been trying to find out ever since.

* * *

Our house was always open to the whole community, during troubles, during feasts — all the time. I thought then that this was a burden because our resources were limited, and my mother and sister and I had to work so hard to accommodate all the guests. I guess I was like Martha grumbling in the kitchen about all that had to be done.

However, when I grew up I recognized the importance of hospitality, and I started doing the same thing in our home. I know it has taken a lot of my energy as a woman who is involved outside the home, but I think now I really value the understanding of hospitality and the sharing of yourself. Unfortunately, many women have lost this kind of understanding because they think they are slaves to the kitchen, or they have more important things to do. By extending hospitality I got to know some of the most interesting people from whom I learned a lot, especially in the area of cross-cultural relations.

I must admit that there were some misunderstandings and frustrations because people come from different cultures and don't understand our ways. When I served two kinds of food just to introduce them to Arab cuisine, they would ask: "Where is the Quaker simplicity?" Others thought that I could do all of this because I didn't have involvements outside the home and was not a "liberated" woman.

They didn't understand that I did it because I believe in it. I think the most important thing I have learned from these experiences is that we have to be very careful to allow our guests space and freedom.

* * *

I didn't get any specific ideas about Jews from my family. I never heard that they were especially good or bad people, but before 1948 I used to hear people say how the wealthiest brides always tried to buy their clothes from Tel Aviv. Or someone would say: "My husband was so concerned that he took me to a Jewish doctor."

There was, however, one thing I was very concerned about: the situation of the refugees. It was simply not just, but this conviction had nothing to do with any mental picture I had about Jews being either bad or good.

Even in our own community the refugees were victimized on every side. Sometimes they accepted work at lower wages, so they were accused of depriving the local people of employment.

If there was one thing all of my family knew, it was that their situation was pathetic, and we always tried to help them by sharing whatever we could — recommending them for education, providing clothes, or offering them work in my father's coffee house.

* * *

I graduated from the Friends Girls' School. Then I wanted to go to Bryn Mawr College because I had been accepted there, but I felt that since my parents already had two children studying in the United States, a third would put too much strain on them. Then my husband came along and we got married. He is also a Quaker, and a pharmacist by profession. In fact, he had taught me chemistry in school.

I was always ambitious, and I started studying on my own. I took many courses through correspondence from Earlham College, a Quaker school in the United States. The professors sent the books, and I wrote papers. All of my studying was done informally and not for any degree, just because I have always loved to learn.

I began to teach ethics at the Friends Boys' School. I saw that religion and ethics were taught by any teacher who happened to have an extra space in their schedule. I also saw what my children were studying, and was very disappointed with the syllabus. I told the teachers and the principal that the school needed to do something more in that field, so they asked me why I didn't do something myself, and that was how I began to teach.

I also started teaching Christian religion, and when Islam was introduced into the curriculum, I tried to emphasize the values that both Islam and Christianity have in common. That was a very exciting programme for me. Now that I am leaving, my daughter is taking over, and she will continue it.

I had four children. The first girl died very young and now the other three are grown-up. I even have one grandchild now. My children have given me a sense of great joy and accomplishment because they are very committed, not only to our community here, but to the world community as well.

It is not easy to live in this situation of occupation. For instance, yesterday my son went to visit two friends in Bethlehem. From 11 o'clock until two in the afternoon, he was sitting in the car at a road block because the military thought there was a bomb next to Rachel's Tomb. We were waiting at home worrying about him, so when he finally came we were very happy. This kind of thing happens all the time, and it is not easy for young people because they are usually less patient than older people.

* * *

We were not ready for war in 1967. Nobody was prepared for it, and when the Israelis bombed Ramallah, we went into the basement next to our house. A bomb fell nearby and the basement door was blown off. My husband was sitting next to the door and was lucky not to have been killed. Two days after the war began, the Israelis occupied Ramallah.

The war and occupation influenced my children in different ways. My oldest son was eight, and when we came home he took his toy guns, and broke all of them with rocks. I had never approved of these toys, but they had been given to him as gifts. He said that these things made people suffer, and he didn't want them any more.

Our daughter had the impression that Israelis made people suffer. She did not want to wear short dresses — this was when mini-skirts were in style, and she did not want to look like the Israeli army girls who wore them. She also would not eat Israeli ice cream. I think she reacted differently because two of her friends were killed by a bomb which fell next to our house, on the orphanage.

* * *

At the beginning I think my encounters with Israelis were not very successful because they were always treating us as the occupier. In order to have a dialogue, one has to share freely and the Israelis were not accustomed to doing that after the occupation began.

One day we had an explosion in the school lab. I think it was in 1970 or 1971. The army officials were concerned that maybe our students were making something illegal, so two or three of them wanted to visit the school. My husband invited them to our home for coffee. They came, and I remember the look on their faces and the kind of conversation we had.

The first thing they said was: "This is the first Arab home that we have seen with flowers in it. The Arabs don't like flowers. Israelis like flowers. We have ten florists in Jerusalem, you have only one florist in Ramallah."

Everyone kept quiet, but I thought I should respond to this. I did not want to have an argument, only a discussion with them. I said: "I beg your pardon; whether we love or do not love flowers should not be any kind of judgment about whether we are good or bad people. You have ten florists in Jerusalem because most of you live in apartment buildings and don't have your own gardens. We live in houses and have gardens around our houses so we don't need the florist. Go and visit the Old City of Jerusalem or Nazareth or any place. Even in the refugee camps, the smallest places will have window boxes of geraniums and roses, even if they have to be planted in rusty milk cans."

I offered them chocolate cake and other things, but when they left they could not even bring themselves to thank us for our family hospitality or our Arab hospitality. They thanked us for our Quaker hospitality. My husband walked out with them, and they told him that he should be careful because his wife was a very radical person.

I remember, during the 1973 war there was a blackout. The military governor and his aide were on our doorstep for more than an hour. They were talking to us about the war, saying how lucky we were to be in the West Bank because it was the safest place, and how they might be in Damascus that night. I smiled and said: "You may be in Damascus tomorrow, but it will not solve the problem. It will make the problems worse, and will not ensure peace." They could not understand what I was talking about because military success was the only kind of success they knew.

* * *

I have had dialogues with many concerned Jews at meetings arranged by the World Council of Churches, and at some meetings held at the Ecumenical Institute at Tantur. I feel there are many Jews who are struggling to change the situation, and are not pleased with everything that is happening.

When I see the Israeli soldiers here hitting children or coming to the school and frightening them because they sing a patriotic song, my heart bleeds for our children, but I also feel that these soldiers are victims of a regime that does not use their full potential. These soldiers are 18 and 19 years old, and should be in the university or doing something other than spending their lives this way. It is not healthy for them, and it is not healthy for us.

I see the linkage between our problem and theirs because the oppressor is no more free than the oppressed. From this viewpoint, I have been able to communicate with some Israelis.

I feel there is one world made for all of us, and we are all children of God. We don't have time to waste. Either we will make the world better or we will blow it up. We cannot do anything by ourselves, and this is why we have to organize all the people who care about this world to work towards promoting peace and justice, development, and human rights — no matter what anyone's religion or nationality is.

* * *

I must say that on rare occasions I have felt understood by Israelis. I think some of them find it difficult, not because they are unable to understand a person like me, but they do not want to accept the fact that there are people who think as I do and who want to solve problems non-violently. Most Israelis have been brainwashed to think that all Palestinians want to kill them, so they find it difficult if not impossible to deal with Palestinians who they think are different.

It's not that I am different. There are many people who think as I do, but when people are brainwashed by the state and their own propaganda, it is very difficult for them to change their way of thinking. They always ask me the same question: "Do you think there are other people like you?" If they hear me speaking in the United States or in Europe, they ask this same question, and I say: "Of course, there are many other people like me."

None of the West Bank residents are fighters. All of us live here without resisting the occupation too violently. It doesn't mean that if you are not violent, you accept the situation. This is where many people misunderstand our struggle for peace.

To try to work for peace non-violently is not a passive thing: it is highly active and very controversial. Some years ago when I spoke in Copenhagen, many Jews came to me and said that I spoke differently and humanely. "We approve of what you said," they told me, "but we think that this is just a strategy planned by the PLO to change their image in the world." Of course that was not the case.

Communication is not easy because of past experiences. When Palestinians and Jews meet, the very situation is a problem. I am the victim and they are the conquerors, so we do not meet on an equal basis. They are defensive because my presence is an embarrassment to them, yet some do listen to me. Whether they understand, I'm not always sure.

We do not fight violently because our ultimate goal is a better society for everyone. We want to get rid of evil and not people. At the beginning,

I did not understand this idea because I thought it meant submission. Now I understand it very well, and I feel compelled to share it especially with young people because they are discovering that non-violence is a very meaningful way of struggling for peace and justice.

I feel it has been a blessing for me to have a religious base. I think I feel freer than most people because I am not limited to one ideology or group which sometimes does not allow one to see the whole picture.

* * *

Unfortunately, I feel a sense of hopelessness among the people who don't think peace is possible. Ten years ago in Nairobi at the World Council's Fifth Assembly, I stood up and said that we Palestinians would accept a state within the 1967 boundaries. This was what I believed then, and I still think it would solve many problems — maybe not all of them, but at least some. Right now this goal is difficult because the Israelis do not feel they have to give up anything. There is no Arab or international power to put pressure on them, so why should they make any movement?

The Israelis cannot even think of the Palestinians having a state because after 19 years the West Bank and the Gaza Strip have become economically and politically important. The religious Jews, think this is the promised land and refuse to give up an inch. Economically, occupying the West Bank has made it possible for Israelis to get a cheap five-room apartment somewhere in the beautiful West Bank countryside, rather than having to live in one expensive room in Jerusalem.

* * *

Palestinians are like all other people in the world. We are educated; we have a rich culture. We have close family relations and a commitment to our community and to the rest of the world. Let me give you an example: on Monday here at the YWCA we are having a day of prayer and fasting in solidarity with the people of South Africa. We are open to the rest of the world, and not blinded by our own suffering.

The number of Israelis killed through acts of terror is very small compared to the number killed in wars. If the Israelis are really concerned about the loss of life, they should have thought ten times before starting the war in Lebanon. Sometimes they use the terrorism excuse because it's simple and easy for the world to understand. But what they are really saying is: "We do not yet accept that the Palestinians exist." They continue to refer to us as "the inhabitants of Judea and Samaria".

In order to solve a problem, you must talk about the real issues. It is difficult for the Israelis to accept the fact that Palestinians exist because then they have to accept the fact that we have rights as people. All along they have convinced their people that the Jews came to an uninhabited land, and made it bloom. Now, after all these years, it is very difficult to go back and admit to themselves that this is not true. When you go to the West Bank settlements, separate roads have been built so you do not see the Arab villages. It is as if the Israelis are trying to block out the Palestinian population from their eyes and minds.

I don't think it is difficult for the Palestinians to accept the presence of Israelis. It is an accomplished fact. We travel on Israeli travel documents, we have Israeli identity cards, we pay Israeli taxes, we buy Israeli goods. It's a reality, but it doesn't mean that this reality should prevent us from existing. The Israelis exist and we want to exist with them as equals.

* * *

When I see the children and look in their faces, I become hopeful. I see in them a power that can make a change. Our daughter is committed to live and teach here. Now she has her own child, and that is also a sign of hope. The young people are telling me that no matter what, life will go on and we should prepare for a better life. This gives me hope.

Another thing that gives me hope is my faith. Sometimes when I sit in the quiet of my room, I know that God knows who I am. God knows me by name. I am as important to God as any other person in the world, and this knowledge gives me a sense of responsibility. Because I am a child of God created in God's image, I have to promote that image. That is my responsibility. It is a blessing, but it is also a responsibility, and this keeps me going. I do have moments of desperation when I think that what I do does not make any difference, but yet I believe in the saying that instead of cursing the darkness, you should keep the lights on.

Amos Gvirtz

Amos Gvirtz, 40, is a member of Kibbutz Shfayim which is located along the Mediterranean coast north of Tel Aviv. As one of Israel's few conscientious objectors, Gvirtz is a pacifist and believes that Palestinian self-determination can be achieved through non-violent methods.

Gvirtz encourages Palestinians to adopt a non-violent strategy of action. In this way, he says, many more Israelis would be willing to lend their support to their struggle for self-determination. "In a non-violent struggle, I am fighting for justice. But if I support the Palestinians' violent struggle, I am a traitor."

Amos Gvirtz is one of the founding members of a recently formed Fellowship of Reconciliation group in Israel and the West Bank.

To become a conscientious objector is no small thing in Israel. I don't remember exactly when I became one, but I do know that at a very young age I was sensitive to what I would call moral things. It just seemed to happen, not because of anything I read or any relationships I had. I could not accept it when children hit each other, and when that happened I tried to stop it. I also remember that when we were children we used to steal watermelons or corn and eat it, but later I couldn't do it any more. Even if I did not steal it myself, I could not bring myself to eat anything if I knew it was stolen.

When I was growing up, my parents did not hit me. Maybe two times my father hit me in all my childhood, but once he gave me another kind of punishment which was a great lesson and I think the first and best non-violent lesson I ever got. I was about ten years old when some other children and I made a fire that went out of control, and the people in the kibbutz were very angry at us. As a punishment my father did not talk to me, and I think that no other punishment in all of my life was as effective as this.

When I was in high school all the students started to think that soon we would go to the army, and my friends used to ask me: "Okay, you will be in the army, you will have a gun in your hand. An Arab will come at you and what will you do?" I said: "I will shoot twice: I will shoot to defend myself, but then I will shoot myself because I cannot live knowing that I killed somebody."

Going into the army was a big tragedy. It was one of the hardest days of my life, but I did not think I could say no. Since I have a problem with my ear, I was lucky not to have been put into a fighting unit.

However, two good things happened to me during the army time. First, I got a book by Natan Hofshi who was one of the founders of the Israeli War Resisters. This was a great help because until then I did not know that there were other people like me in this country.

The second thing concerned a conflict about some confiscated lands in the Galilee. One of the people who protested against the confiscation was arrested, and the newspapers reported that he also was a conscientious objector. These two things gave me confidence because I found out that I was not alone.

The problem was that I was afraid to say how I really felt because I didn't know what the reaction would be. Finally I asked the army to send me to a small kibbutz for the rest of the military time. I had to meet different officers and have discussions so they could find out if I was really a pacifist or not. In the end they allowed me to go the kibbutz, and I did the rest of my military service there.

Then the problem was about my reserve duty. I had a very long discussion about it because I wanted to do civil service. My point was that since everyone had to serve, I didn't want special favours, but I wanted to do civilian, not military service. The army compromised, but I still had to do my service within the army. After seven years we finally agreed that I would serve in a half-civilian/half-military organization which is supposed to take care of civilian matters in war time, for example, being sure that food is delivered to markets and water is available.

I served my reserve duty on the condition that I didn't handle weapons, that I didn't wear a uniform, that I received orders from a civilian authority, and that I didn't have to serve in the occupied territories. Unfortunately the army and I have differences in understanding the agreement.

Personally, it was a very hard time. I was lucky to have a very tolerant family and society around me. The people here did not want to throw me out of the kibbutz, and when I said that I would leave, they tried very hard to convince me to stay. My mother was the peace-maker of the family. Because of her my ideological differences never hurt the relationships within our family. No one broke off relations or became angry with me.

I was very lucky compared to some other conscientious objectors here. I do know some people who were thrown into prison and broken there, and as a result they finally agreed to serve.

* * *

I was born here in the kibbutz. My mother came from Samarkand, Bukhara, now part of the USSR. My father came from a Polish family that lived in England. They were both part of the socialist youth group that started this kibbutz and were married here. I have spent all of my life in the kibbutz except for two years when I was away working with children with social problems.

I know my father had very good relationships with Arabs. He respected them and wanted to know and learn about them. Since I was born only two years before independence, I saw very few Arabs in my childhood, but I am sure that I never heard a racist remark from either of my parents.

Once or twice when I was growing up our school visited an Arab village, but those were not serious contacts. My real contacts with Arabs began with my non-violent activities. The first was in 1973 when I was in the Israeli section of War Resisters International. Together with an anti-fascist German group we organized an international work camp in an Arab village. I was there for three weeks, and this was the most serious experience I had ever had with Arab people.

There were many problems in this village. I was not very knowledgeable at the time, but could see there the problems that all Arabs have in Israel. The village was a mixed society of Muslims and Christians; there were some original citizens and the others were refugees who had been chased out of their villages in 1948. There were a lot of inner-village conflicts, and that affected my relationships with the people. Because of these conflicts I began to understand how and why the Arabs are divided.

In this village most of the people politically supported the Zionist parties. Three years later I happened to be in a village which did not support the Zionist parties, and I could see how different it was. Since then I have related more to the latter group because it was very strange to hear people politically justify policies that are basically not in their interest. I think, however, that this is always the way minorities are divided. There are those who support the powerful in order to get some advantages, and there are those who oppose the powerful.

I can understand why this happens. I don't know how I would behave if I were in this kind of minority situation so I am not in the position to judge. It was clear that those who supported the Zionist parties feared that they would be accused of betraying the Arab cause, and most of the people could not understand why a person like me who has everything he needs and lives in a kibbutz should come to their village to help.

There were some things about Arab society that I didn't like, for example, the situation of the women and children. These were things that were hard for me to accept. They can say it is none of my business, but I am only seeing it from my point of view.

* * *

My main contacts with Palestinians now come through my peace activities. I am active in a group called the Jewish/Arab Action Committee for Jaffa Arabs, which tries to help the Jaffa Arabs fight for their rights. With this group I have tried to develop the idea of what I call "constructive protest".

Usually our protests take the form of demonstrations, petitions, and sometimes writing letters to newspapers. But to take a demonstration as an example, we always must ask what we are doing. We are opposing an authority in order to demand that they do what we think they should do, but after that we go home and our responsibility ends. In a constructive protest we search for ways to take responsibility to see that at least some of what we demand happens.

In Jaffa most of the Arabs live in poor neighbourhoods. The authorities want to destroy these poor areas and rebuild them for more wealthy people. The idea is to change the situation in Tel Aviv where the wealthy people live in the north and the poor in the south. They want to bring some wealthy people to the south, and Jaffa seems to be a good place since it is close to the sea and has a good view which is appealing to most people.

To me this seems to be just another case of pushing Arabs away from their homes, and this is the central point of the Israeli-Palestinian conflict. We Jews came and pushed many Arabs away from their lands and built our own homes on this land. I believe that peace will not be achieved until we stop this process and find some kind of a compromise.

Since the authorities want the Arabs to leave that area, they deliver very poor municipal services. There is infrequent garbage collection. The sidewalks, if there are any, are in bad condition, and education is of a very low quality.

Our group organized international work camps to clean the streets, make gardens, renovate houses, and just try to encourage people to stay and put pressure on the authorities to change their policies. We saw some very slow change after our first camp in 1983 because the next year there were garbage cans in the streets, and the city did some street cleaning. Now the authorities have agreed to allow some of the people to renovate their houses or make some additions. We hope that this work will bring about some changes.

* * *

I believe that those who are opposing peace in Israel are creating what I call "facts of war". Every settlement built in the occupied territories, every confiscation of land, is creating a "fact of war".

We in the peace movement haven't found ways of creating "facts of peace". We are always protesting, but instead of only being critical, we must also create something that will contribute to peace. For example, in Jaffa there are Arabs and Jews who teach children after school because the educational situation for Arabs can be horrible. This is what I call constructive protest.

Now my main work is with a group called Arabs and Jews for Non-Violence, Fellowship and Peace, whose main goal is to introduce nonviolent protest into this conflict. We are working in cooperation with the Palestinian Centre for the Study of Non-Violence, which was founded by a Palestinian named Mubarak Awad. So far our actions have always been in cooperation with that centre, and in the style of constructive, nonviolent protest. We have had four actions and only one of them was a demonstration.

The first action was in a village called Katana where the Israeli authorities wanted to take over land belonging to some Arab farmers, and in the process they uprooted about 2,000 olive trees. Our group of Palestinians, Jews, and expatriots went there and planted other olive trees. The authorities came and uprooted these, but for us this was a way of creating a fact of peace.

One of the ways the authorities take land from Arabs is by enforcing an old law which says that if land is not cultivated for so many years, the owners lose their right to it. So we go and plant trees in some of these fields to prove that the land is a cultivated plot.

One of our last actions occurred recently when we went to visit some shops in Hebron. The Israeli army has built a big fence in front of these shops. They claim that the fence provides security for the Gush Emunim settlers who are living above the shops, but this means that people who want to come into the shops are thoroughly searched before entering. Obviously, a lot of people don't like this, and they go to other shops. The shopkeepers lose business, and some of them may be forced to close and move away, which is just what the settlers want. In order to encourage the shopkeepers to stay, we decided to go there and do some shopping.

As in our other actions, we faced the military so beforehand we gave very strict orders to keep the non-violent atmosphere. We always make it clear to the soldiers that we are not fighting them or the settlers as persons, instead we are struggling against the evil that they are doing.

* * *

Most of us don't remember that this conflict has killed thousands of people, and thousands of others have been physically and mentally wounded. People have lost their homes and are permanently suffering under occupation. Usually we measure things in dollars, but our non-violent group measures in terms of human suffering. We see that if this conflict continues, it will only create more victims and more suffering. We are not advocating passiveness, but are searching for those methods which will carry on the struggle without creating more suffering for anybody.

If the Palestinians had enough real power to violently defeat Israel, it would cause so much suffering that in the end the victory would be worth nothing. We believe that at the moral level the Palestinians have power, maybe even more than the Israelis, and therefore non-violent struggle can be much more effective than violence.

We are not a purely pacifist group. Personally I am a pacifist, but that is not a condition for joining. The only condition is belief in non-violence. We think that in every conflict situation each side has some kind of violent or non-violent power against the other.

The most unequal power situation I can think of was the situation of the Jews against the Nazis in the Holocaust period. When I think of those who tried to rebel against Nazi power, I see that they had no chance of final success because the difference in power was too great. Would the Jews have had any success using non-violent methods? Again I must say that they had no possibility to succeed. So where was their power? It was in making their own decision about where they were going to die. They could decide not to die in Auschwitz where the Nazis wanted them to die or they could force the Nazis to kill them in Warsaw.

Now I don't know if I would be so brave. It is not fair to sit here comfortably and judge anybody. I don't know if I would have taken up weapons, but theoretically the non-violent answer would have been to say to the Nazis: "I have decided that I do not want to die where you want me to die."

* * *

The Palestinians have a much better situation. First, they don't face Nazis. If I try to see the nature of our conflict, I usually compare it with the conflict between the Red Indians and the white people in America. Both here and there one people came into another's territory, and in the historical process many of the original inhabitants were pushed away from their homes. It is a very basic kind of conflict; you can see the same thing in Australia.

However, there are differences. The Red Indians did not work for the white people. Here, from the very beginning, Palestinians worked for Jewish people, and that made them very dependent. But Israel is dependent too; it depends on the cheap Palestinian work force. This fact increases the Palestinians' potential power for non-violent struggle since Israel needs them for a labour force and as a consumer market. If the Palestinians non-violently refuse to play that role, they can exert power and can also appeal to Israel's conscience. So far our actions have been more to appeal to the conscience and show where injustice has occurred. We want to create facts of peace, but also to point out injustice.

The Palestinians could use the boycott method and refuse to work for the Israelis and use Israeli products, but for this they must be very well organized. Not long ago I had an interesting discussion with a Jewish woman from South Africa who was with the African National Congress. She told me that they had tried non-violence but it had not worked. I asked if they had tried a general strike. She said they had, but it had failed. I asked if the general strike had failed, or if they had failed in calling the strike. She said it was the latter.

What does it mean to call for a general strike? You must have prepared alternatives for the people so they will not die of hunger. Gandhi prepared the alternative. He told the people to work in their homes, not to sell cotton to the British, but to spin it at home and make a living from that. Only after he provided an economic alternative did things start to work.

* * *

When I think of that village of Katana or those shopkeepers in Hebron, I believe they have certain options: to be passive, to choose to respond violently, or to employ the non-violent struggle.

To be passive helps nobody except the oppressor. If the Palestinians choose the violent struggle, they will be alone, but if they choose a non-violent struggle, they will have Jewish people and foreigners to support them. As an Israeli I can participate in a non-violent struggle because my existence is not threatened by it. In a non-violent struggle I am fighting for justice, but if I support the Palestinians' violent struggle, I am a traitor.

If we Jews had no security fears, I believe that many of us would be ready to recognize the rights of the Palestinians, but every terror action increases Israeli fear that a Palestinian state will be just another step towards the end of Israel. Because of this fear we refuse to recognize the rights of the Palestinians and prefer to hold the occupied territories. Non-violent struggle could reduce this fear, and it's another area where the Palestinians can help the Israelis. Israelis who are aware of injustices done to Palestinians can support their rights, but if it were to be a non-violent struggle, they would be able more actively to support the Palestinians.

* * *

If you consider countries that have become independent in the last thirty years, only a few remain democracies, like India and Israel. There is a level of democracy in Israel because the Jews were democratically organized before the British left.

India is the most complicated country in the world; it makes Lebanon look like a child's game, but it survives as a democracy. Why? Because of the way India struggled against the British. Gandhi created a new political culture through the non-violent struggle. Not that everyone was a pacifist like Gandhi, but the Indians were influenced and are still influenced by him, otherwise India would have blown up long ago.

I believe that Palestinian terror hurts them more than it hurts us. It creates internal Palestinian conflicts, and because of that I'm afraid of two things: first, if the Palestinians do get their state, they could end up with a terrible dictatorship that would not allow any differences of opinion, and would turn into a new oppressive power. Secondly, they could find themselves living through a series of assassinations of leaders. However, if they achieve their state through non-violent struggle, it could completely alter the picture. Non-violence not only helps us to help them, but it also helps them help themselves.

* * *

We are a very small organization, and our role is to bring this non-violent option to people's attention so they will begin to understand it. If you speak of a violent way to solve problems, you have a very clear idea of what those tools are. However, when you talk about the tools of non-violence, it is very unclear, and that is one of the greatest difficulties we have — to explain what our tools are. We have to communicate much more than ideas; people must begin to understand the tools of non-violence as well as they understand the tools of violence.

In our first action at Katana we faced the army, the police, and the "Green Patrol" which functions as the Ministry of Agriculture's police force. All of these people are paid a salary to do what they do; this is their job. And who are we? We are just some people who, after our regular work, go to protest injustice. How can we confront this huge system? What do we have on our side? I think we have the moral power to open people's eyes to injustice; it is a power that generates its own power to affect people's consciences.

I am fighting not because I feel I have the chance to change things, but because I don't want to be like a sheep that is led to the slaughter. I was in Germany during the protests over the Pershing II missiles, and at the gate of an army base I heard an interesting conversation between one of the protesters and an American soldier. The protester was asking him why he was helping to prepare for the nuclear holocaust. The soldier said: "Look, it is not in my hands. I cannot affect it. I can't change anything. I do my service and go home."

Here was a person who protects these missiles and says he can't do anything. He has a gun in his hand, but he can very easily go like a sheep to the slaughter just like hundreds of thousands of soldiers have been killed in wars they did not understand. They killed and died because they got orders, not because they wanted to kill or be killed. They didn't understand what it was all about, they didn't protest, they just helplessly and powerlessly went to their deaths. We have to make people aware that they do have power, and that non-violent power does change things.

Mustafa Natshe

Until 1929, Jews had lived in the West Bank city of Hebron for centuries. That year the Arab population rioted, a number of Jews were killed, and the rest fled the city.

Since 1967, when settlers first began efforts to re-establish a Jewish presence in Hebron, the city has again been the scene of violence and bloodshed. After six Jews were murdered there in May 1980, Mayor Fahd Kawasmeh was deported by Israeli military authorities even though no connection was made between him and the murders.

*With the deportation of Kawasmeh, deputy mayor **Mustafa Natshe** became acting mayor of Hebron. Later, after another settler was stabbed, the Israeli authorities deposed Natshe.*

Today Natshe, 55, is recognized as one of the West Bank's most prominent political leaders. In 1983, after six people were killed in a bus bombing in Jerusalem, Natshe, along with four other West Bank leaders, publicly condemned the act on the front page of the East Jerusalem newspaper, al-Fajr.

I was born in Hebron and my family has lived in this area for more than one thousand years. I went to elementary and secondary school here, and then I studied chemical engineering at Cairo University. After graduating in 1956, I returned and worked here in Hebron.

My political career began with the 1976 municipal elections when I was elected deputy mayor of Hebron. After Mayor Kawasmeh was deported in May 1980, I was acting mayor until 7 July when the Israeli military authorities deposed both me and the city's elected council.

* * *

Before 1948 my contacts with Jews were very positive. I had business relationships with them, and they were very friendly towards me. I used to travel a lot to Jerusalem and Jaffa because my family had an orchard of 170 dunams near a Jewish settlement called Ramat Hasharon. In 1948 we lost that land along with the property we had in Jerusalem.

After 1967, Jewish settlers decided to begin living in the centre of Hebron. A lot of Israelis were against this because Hebron is such a densely populated Arab city, and they thought that having Jewish settlers here would make the situation more difficult and in the end the settlers would be an obstacle to peace. These people came to Hebron to demonstrate against the settlers, and to show their solidarity with us. It was from that time that I began to have a relationship with the Israeli peace movement, and it is a relationship that has continued, especially after 1980 when I became the acting mayor.

When the settlers would harass Arabs, the peace-lovers, as I call them, would come to show their solidarity. I remember once in 1981 when some settlers threw bombs at an Arab widow's house because they wanted to take her land which was near the settlement of Kyriat Arba. About 65 Israeli cars of the "Peace Now" movement came to her house to show their solidarity. They came again when the settlers demolished the electric pylons which carried electricity to Arab houses.

Recently about ten members of the Israeli Knesset met with us at the Park Hotel here in Hebron. They came to protest the Tehyia political convention being held at Kyriat Arba. Usually Israeli political parties have their conventions in Jerusalem, and then after the first day they go to Tel Aviv for the second and third days. Tehyia, which is a very right-wing, anti-Arab party, held the first day of their convention in Jerusalem, but then they came to Kyriat Arba for the second and third days. They did this to give the impression that all of the land in the West Bank belongs to Israel and the Jewish people.

At the convention they called for the expulsion of 1½ million Arabs from the West Bank, and when some of the Knesset members heard this, they decided to protest against these fascist ideas by coming to the hotel to meet with us and speak about peace. When they arrived they were met by Jewish settlers who shouted at them, pushed them about, and threw stones trying to prevent them from meeting with us.

* * *

You can see that since the settlers came, the situation in the centre of Hebron has changed very much. Many of the Arab families left because of continuous harassment by the military authorities who are trying to protect the settlers. They make life so difficult for the Arab population that many people just leave. In the end the settlers achieve their goal of getting the Arabs to move so that more and more settlers can come in.

If any incident occurs, a curfew is imposed in the centre of the city. The people who are living there are mostly poor, and they depend on daily work to get food. If there is a curfew, they can't get food so they decide to move outside the centre to avoid the curfew.

Secondly, the authorities moved the Central Bus Station from the centre to the border of the city. Here in Hebron there are two basic elements of daily life: the Central Bus Station and the wholesale vegetable market. This is an agricultural area, and the small farmers bring their produce on the buses and sell it at the market which is near the station. From there they go to the butcher to buy their meat, and then they go back to their villages by bus. Their life depends upon the bus station and the market.

The military authorities tried to move the bus station when I was the mayor. They closed it by military order, and I went to the Supreme Court in Jerusalem with an appeal. When I won the appeal, they were obliged to reopen the station. So what did they do? One month later they deposed both me and the city council. They appointed an Israeli who said he was the mayor, and he didn't want the bus station in the centre of the city so he moved it away.

They also tried to move the wholesale vegetable market from the city centre. To do this they closed off the entrances to the market — all five of them — with concrete and steel. They said they did this because of security reasons, but this is nonsense. They just want to get rid of the Arab population from the centre of the city so that more Jewish settlers can move in.

* * *

When any incident occurs, the settlers take the law into their own hands, and the way the Israeli army deals with them is completely different from the way they deal with the Arab population. For example, when the settlers were throwing stones at the Knesset members who were trying to meet with us at the hotel, the soldiers said: "Please don't do this. Please move out of the way."

On the very same day Arab students from the Polytechnic Institute also demonstrated against the Tehyia convention. In this case 250 Israeli soldiers attacked the Institute and threw about 110 cannisters of tear gas. They also beat the students brutally. Five were seriously injured and sent to the hospital. The others were arrested and sent to prison. So you see the difference between how the Israeli army treats the Jewish settlers and how they treat the local Arab population.

* * *

I was deposed as acting mayor because the military authorities said that I didn't cooperate with them after a settler was stabbed in the city. They also said that I didn't facilitate a way for the settlers to move into the city, that I didn't provide them with electricity, water, etc. They also said that I brought in funds from enemy sources to build schools, open roads, and generate electricity and water for different projects in the city. Finally, they said that I annoyed the authorities by going to the Supreme Court.

I told them that it was our right not to encourage settlers to come to the centre of the city, especially since in such a highly populated Arab city, this is just asking for trouble.

The funds they said I got from enemy sources came from Saudi Arabia and Jordan, but the Israelis had approved this. In fact, we gave them a full accounting of how much we got and exactly what we did with it. It was spent for the welfare of the people, and we are proud to have been given Arab funds especially since the Israelis collect taxes from us and give us almost nothing by way of municipal services. And, I told them, I had a right to take my grievances to the Supreme Court.

* * *

Before the Balfour Declaration there were no distinctions here between Jews and Arabs or between Muslims, Christians and Jews. In 1917 there were 70,000 Jews in Palestine and 700,000 Arabs. The Arabs possessed 98 percent of the land, and the Jews had 2 percent. Of course the Balfour Declaration promised a homeland to the Jews, but it also contained a promise not to harm the rights of the people who were already living here.

I believe that the situation can be solved in a peaceful way. The Arabs can have their state, and the Israelis theirs. The Arabs want to live in their state, side by side, and in peace with Israel.

With two states, if Jews say they wish to live in Hebron, okay. There were Jews living in Hebron until 1929, and they will be welcome again to live here, but they will live in a Palestinian state. There are also Arabs living in Israel so we don't mind. But we don't want the fanatical Jews who say that this land is the Land of Israel given only to them by God and because of that we don't have any rights here. We are willing, really, to live in peace, but not as a nation occupied by another.

We accept any security regulation, but they must apply to both sides. Israelis claim that a Palestinian state will threaten Israel, but we say the opposite. Israel has more armed strength than all the neighbouring Arab states, so we feel Israel threatens the security of the Arab states. Security regulations must affect both sides.

* * *

The occupation forces here call us terrorists, but isn't it right for the Palestinians to struggle for their human rights? Of course such a struggle must avoid making innocent people victims of its violence, but the Israelis behaved in the same way before 1948 when they blew up the King David Hotel and 70 people died, not all of whom were British soldiers.

We condemn terror. Attacking the airports in Rome or Vienna — this we completely condemn. But we also wish to say that it is not only terror when you kill somebody. It is also terror when you kill a person in an indirect way. For example, if you dismiss farmers and confiscate their land, what does this mean? It means that, in a way, you kill the farmers because farming is their only source of income. If you demolish an Arab's house, what does it mean? If you deport a person, what does it mean? All of such actions are obstacles to peace.

* * *

I feel that I am really understood by Israelis. Many of them do understand that we must have our national rights as they have theirs. They also understand that we must have our own state.

For example, last week one of the Israeli peace-lovers came to visit the old Jewish quarter here where until 1929 his grandfather had lived. German television had an interview with him, a Jewish settler, and me. The peace-lover and I shared the same ideas, and he said to the settler: "Look, you have just come to this area. I have roots in Hebron, and I want the Arabs to have their right to live as a nation."

Of course the settler did not recognize us as a nation, and said that we Palestinians can only have our rights as individuals. He said that all of the land of Israel is the Promised Land because it was given to the Jews by God.

Many Israelis are willing, really, to make peace. If they would stop building settlements and confiscating land, the PLO could also say that they would stop the armed struggle for a period of time in order to create a quiet atmosphere so negotiations could begin.

* * *

We are sometimes pessimistic here because we think that the Israelis are not willing to make the effort for peace. I say the Israeli government, not the Israeli people because there are many of them who wish to cooperate in order to achieve peace, but I think that the Israeli government is not ready. They want peace and all of the land at the same time.

There is a part of the Qu'ran that we should always remember. It says: God created you as nations and tribes in order to understand each other — not to quarrel, but to understand.

We must make the effort to understand. It is the only hope we have.

Ibrahim Sim'an

Ibrahim Sim'an *is a 46 year-old Baptist clergyman who lives in Haifa. Describing himself as a "Christian, Arab, Palestinian, Israeli", Sim'an says that having only one of those identities in Israel is difficult enough. Having all four is almost impossible. "When a refugee camp is bombarded, I am first a Palestinian," he says. "When an innocent Israeli is killed, I am first an Israeli. In all cases, I try to be a human being."*

Sim'an's ideas have been greatly influenced by the Israeli pacifist, Joseph Abeliah, and as a result he favours a programme of non-violent struggle for both Israeli Arab and Palestinian rights. Politically, Sim'an is a member of the Citizens' Rights Party and serves on its Central Committee.

On the whole, Arab citizens of Israel are not well treated. I have always thought that this is a terrible hindrance to co-existence because if we really mean business when we speak about peace, it has to begin at home. Unless the model of peaceful co-existence is established here in Israel between the Jewish majority and the Arab minority, Israel cannot convince the Arab states that it really wants peace.

Choosing to stay in this country obliges me as an Israeli citizen to be loyal to the laws of the state. The name Israeli Arab sounds very strange. I am a Christian, Arab, Palestinian, Israeli. To be one of these four in Israel is quite difficult; to be all four at the same time is almost impossible. It can be a paralyzing process unless you can find some kind of self-therapy to help you cope with it. Being an Israeli and a Palestinian puts you in the awkward situation of sometimes having your state at war with your own people, and with whom do you stand?

I experienced near-total paralysis during the outbreak of the Lebanon war in 1982. I sat by the radio and heard the news that the Israeli army was fighting in Lebanon, and that the Phalangists were aiding them against the Palestinians.

Two of my neighbours were serving in the Israeli army. One of them was newly married, and I could not look into the eyes of his wife when she passed on her way to work, knowing that her husband was facing the possibility of either "kill or be killed".

And yet being a Palestinian, I also knew that my people were in the situation of "kill or be killed", and for them it was mostly be killed. All of the elements that were fighting each other in Lebanon were also fighting inside of me. Finally I got myself together and telephoned the Rambam Hospital and asked if there were any wounded people being brought in from Lebanon. They said there were. I told them that I was a Baptist minister, and I was here to help out if there was anything that I could do.

Within 36 hours I organized help from churches, and arranged for some guest houses to receive the families of these wounded people. I got the keys to the apartment of a Jewish friend who was away, and accommodated some people who were visiting the wounded. Through the churches I recruited some teams of volunteers from all over — Germans, Americans and Arabs. Surprisingly, two women came from the West Bank, and were more than willing to help even the Phalangist wounded.

Later on I organized a public committee which began offering help to refugee camps. We collected aid — nearly 70 tons of clothing, a few thousand pairs of winter boots for children, some 2,000 kerosene heaters, some rations and vitamins and other things which were donated from as far away as the labour unions in Austria. We collected over $45,000 for a school building in the Ein Hilweh refugee camp.

I do what I do to reduce people's suffering because people who are hurt are only people who are hurt. Regardless of their political identity, they are human beings, and the ability to hold out a hand to help them makes you forget about your nationalistic, political identity and turns you towards your human identity.

I say that when a refugee camp is bombarded, I am first a Palestinian. When an innocent Israeli is killed, I am first an Israeli. In all cases, I try to be a human being.

* * *

I was born in the midst of the Second World War in a village near Haifa. My family fled Haifa and went to that village during the few German bombardments in 1940.

The family is very dispersed. Three or four generations ago our ancestors had left Aleppo in Syria. One of them came to Palestine, another went to Jordan, a third went to Lebanon, and one remained in Syria. During the following generations communication was not easy, and we lost contact with many of the relatives.

After 400 years of Turkish imperialism, there was real poverty here. The land was poor and there was little or no health care. My grandfather died as a young man, and when my father was 12 years old he was forced to be responsible for a large family of five brothers and sisters. He left the village where he was born near Nazareth, and moved to Haifa because there were more possibilities for work. At that time you couldn't live if you had only one job, so he became a jack-of-all-trades. He worked in construction and mechanics, was a pipefitter in the oil refineries, and for most of his life was a house painter.

* * *

You might say that my becoming a Baptist was very much an accident. When I finished primary school it was time to choose my secondary school, but my family could not afford to pay tuition, because in the public schools you had to pay the whole year's tuition at the beginning of the term. At private schools, like the Baptist school, you could pay monthly instalments which made it a lot easier, so that is why I ended up going to the Baptist school even though our family was and is Greek Orthodox.

Until 1955 I had been involved with the Communist Youth Organization, and I went to the Baptist school with that background. It took me more than a semester to pour all of my atheistic questions on the poor religion teacher. I intended to embarrass him and show the class his ignorance, but through it all he kept smiling. He had tremendous patience and used to say: "I don't promise that I can answer all your questions, but let's look for answers in God's word together."

Then I had a vision. One night when I was half asleep I heard a noise, and when I opened my eyes, I saw Jesus being crucified. I said to myself that this was a dream and went back to sleep. Again came the same noise, and then a third time. I started to cry, and then I saw Jesus lift up his right arm, point it at me and say: "Why are you crying? You should rejoice, this is being done for you. Go and tell others."

The very next morning I went to the religion teacher and told him about this vision. Since he was a deacon of the church and used to preach at various places around Nazareth, he told me that I should tell people about this vision. I was 16 years old then, and since that time I have tried to live up to Jesus' call.

* * *

I remember the time around 1948 very well because I had a cousin who was killed in an ambush. He was a student at Terra Sancta College in Jerusalem, and on his way home to us, the bus was ambushed and he was hit by six bullets. By the time he was taken to the English Hospital in Nazareth, he had lost too much blood and he died. He was 17 years old.

I also remember the riots at the oil refineries in Haifa where my father was a pipefitter. Some of the Arab workers attacked their Jewish co-workers and killed many of them. I remember my father saying how lucky he was not to have been working that day because he was getting medical treatment in Nazareth. That was the week that he decided we should move to Nazareth because of the violence in Haifa.

One of my father's best friends was killed in a riot in Haifa. I was seven, and I climbed up to the window to see his body, and his chest was just like a net because there were so many bullet holes in it. I never forgot that, and I think that was the first time I began to ask questions about why all of this was happening.

I remember when in 1948 Arab propaganda said that we had won the city of Safed, and it was supposed to be the temporary capital of Palestine. Soldiers from the Arab armies began shooting in the air, but within an hour we found out that the opposite had happened, and that the Jews had taken over. So many people were disappointed, and a few even spoke of suicide.

Soon barefoot women and children began coming into Nazareth from the nearby villages and also from cities like Tiberias and Beit She'an. Their feet were bleeding and they had lost everything other than what they could carry with them.

I remember how some of the Arab armies imposed themselves on the Palestinian population. They came to the villages and asked for the best food, for chicken, for hot bread; nobody could say no, even though they didn't have enough for themselves.

The Jordanian army tried to take my father into custody because he had an old hunting gun and they wanted him to go to battle with it. He was nearly forced to use most of the money he saved from his work at the oil refineries to buy a gun. These are all terrible memories.

* * *

On the first anniversary of the state of Israel, we Palestinians were forced to celebrate independence day. We were given small Israeli flags, and were taken to march before some of Israel's ministers who were visiting Nazareth. That was what led me to join the Communist Youth because there we were told that the Israelis were a force of occupation. This was not our independence, it was our tragedy.

In 1954, I was invited to spend a summer vacation in a kibbutz. We were supposed to work four hours a day, and have three or four hours of Hebrew lessons. I went to Kibbutz Shamrat which is not far from Acre. The members of this kibbutz were concentration camp survivors, and our Hebrew lessons took the form of conversations and sharing of experiences. That was a very traumatic experience for me.

After that I was totally convinced of the Jewish right to a certain corner of the world which they could claim as their home. But at the same time, I could not understand why Jewish independence should have to come at the expense of my people. Wasn't there any way to satisfy the national aspirations of both peoples? Did the leadership of both peoples spend enough time and energy looking for solutions which would not deprive either the Jews or Palestinians of their national hopes? I understood that the Jews deserved a homeland of their own, but I thought the Palestinians deserved nothing less.

One has to realize that the state of Israel is here to stay. I think that it is a waste of energy, resources and human lives to try and change this fact, but I do think that not enough has been done to satisfy the aspirations of the original, local inhabitants of Palestine — meaning my own people.

* * *

At the beginning of the 1967 war, something strange happened to me in a bus. It was overcrowded so I couldn't move, and in front of me was a mother with a baby in her arms. I began looking into the baby's eyes, and all of a sudden I began to see questions in its eyes: "Why should my father be fighting now?" Soon I began to see thousands of other eyes on both sides of the border asking the same questions, and the noise was so loud it almost made me faint. I couldn't bear it, and when the bus reached the stop where I was to get off, I did not notice it.

Why should this woman be widowed, I thought. Why should other women on the other side of the border be widowed? In whose favour is this? What interest does it serve to fight, kill, or be killed? I think that

after my calling to the Christian ministry, this was my second calling —
to be a peace-maker.

Together with Dr Rachel Rosensweig I helped established a group
called "Partnership" which deals with Arab-Jewish relationships within
Israel. We based the organization on three main assumptions: first, that
there are common interests that need to be encouraged and publicized;
second, that there is a need to develop mutual trust between Arabs and
Jews so that they can commmunicate; and third, that these relations
should encourage individual self-esteem.

On one occasion we had arranged a seminar for Jewish and Arab kids,
and just 24 hours before the event was to take place, I got a call from one
of the Jewish counsellors who said her kids had decided not to come. We
had rented a bus; the place was reserved, and everything was set up. So
together with a Jewish colleague of mine, I went to speak to these kids to
try and find out what the problem was.

I began by explaining what the Partnership programme was, what it
meant to be partners, why it was necessary to be partners, how it is our
destiny as Arabs and Jews to live together in peace, and why it is
important to know each other's viewpoints, customs, traditions, mentality
and so on. Then I decided to go around the circle and ask each person why
he or she did not want to go to the seminar.

The person who volunteered to speak first was a big boy about 15 years
old. He appeared to be the leader of the group; he had the biggest body
and the longest tongue. "Why should I go," he said, "I hate Arabs. They
need to be thrown into the ocean. They are all terrorists and I don't need
to know them. Today they can be friends, but tomorrow they will stab me
in the back. Who needs such friends?"

While he was saying all this I kept smiling. When he finished, he
thought I would answer right away, but I just said: "Next? Who would
like to speak next?"

The next person was a girl about the age of my daughter and she said:
"Well, I'm hesitant. I feel that I am in the midst of a circle of fear, but
being surrounded by it makes me feel secure. I'm afraid to burst out."

"I understand you," I said, "and I think my daughter used to feel the
same way you do. Would you do me a favour? Here is our telephone
number. Could you call my daughter and ask her how she felt before she
went to meet Jews. I know that Arab girls are more conservative than
you, but somehow she got over it. Would you just talk to her? Whether or
not you go to this seminar, you may be encouraged, and you might even
have the chance to meet her."

We went round the circle and then I came back to this big boy and asked: "Do you know why I came this evening?"

"No," he said. "It's only because I care about you," I answered. "I think I came out of love for you. Is that the way to repay me for this love? Why do you hate me?"

"I was not talking about you," he said. "But I am one of those Arabs who you say you hate," I replied. "And I promise you that there are thousands of other Arabs who are far better than I am. How can you speak in such general terms? Can you say for sure that all Jews are a hundred percent good? Do you think that all Jews have clear consciences about everything that has been done to the Arabs?"

"I was not talking about you," he said again.

"Listen," I said, "all it will cost you is 60 pounds for this seminar. I will pay you the 60 pounds plus 20 pounds pocket money, but only if you go to the seminar and promise *not* to change your views. Once you change, you have to pay all of it back."

He looked straight at me and said: "I could change and hide it, and not tell you."

"Man," I said, "you have already changed. What's your name?"

"It's Berko... short for Berkowitz."

"You were born to be a big Berko," I said, "so why choose to be a little Meir Kahane?"

The guy bought the idea, and when he was convinced, twenty other kids came along, and it was one of the most successful seminars we ever had.

Relationships are always a risky business, but isn't it a big risk to plan for war? Is there a guarantee that every time you go to war, you will be the winner? With all of America's technology, do you think that it did a good job in Vietnam? Building relationships is a big risk, but once you trust yourself and you trust the other, I think in spite of the risk, you give yourself and the other person the chance to take a well-calculated risk for peace, rather than a terribly calculated risk for war.

During the 1973 war, one of my neighbours had her husband and two sons on the front. She began to complain that the Arabs would be happy if all the Jews were killed, and so on and so forth. I heard her but did not respond.

On the second night of the war, I saw that there was some kind of trouble with the electricity and her house had no lights. I was sure she did not know how to change a fuse, so I took my ladder and screw-driver and went and fixed the fuse so she could have light. It seemed that my response brought light not only to her house, but to her heart as well. She began dealing with us in a very different way, and started coming to me with her problems, small and big.

* * *

What keeps me doing what I'm doing? Well, first I think that if we lose hope, we stop living. If you get deep into despair and lose your last bit of hope, then you are dead. I haven't lost hope yet. True, there are many times when I get very angry, angry at the whole world, but I deal with it. At times like that I don't mix with people. I come up to this room, lock myself in and pour my anger out on paper. That usually cleans out my system.

I have wept on several occasions. One of them was when I took my first trip to Europe. I went by plane to Switzerland and Munich, and went from there to Austria by train. When we crossed the border we could not even feel it. The border police came into the train and asked if there were any tourists who had visas, and if I had not said a word, nobody would have approached me. I wept because I knew that if I would even get near the border here, I would be shot by both Israelis and Arabs.

Once I was giving a lecture and began by asking if there was a psychologist or psychiatrist in the audience. One person held up his hand, and I said: "What would you tell somebody who is a Palestinian but living in Israel, who is an Arab but not a Muslim, an Israeli but not a Jew, a Christian but not a Roman Catholic or a Greek Orthodox, and a Protestant but not an Anglican. What would you tell such a person?"

"I'd tell him to go on living," he said. And that is what I intend to do.

Edna Zaretsky

Edna Zaretsky, 44, is a Haifa-born sociologist and educator. Originally her work involved leadership training for disadvantaged Jewish youth, but when approached to include Arab youngsters in her training programmes, she began developing models and materials for Arab-Jewish youth encounters.

A good deal of Zaretsky's work is aimed at breaking down the stereotypes Jews and Arabs have of each other. "All my life I have worked in education," she says, "but because I am also a sociologist, I doubt that education alone can change the world. However, after every workshop I do, I see changes in people."

Most recently Zaretsky has been involved in a Haifa University research project to assess Jewish and Arab attitudes about co-existence in Israel. The results, which are yet to be published, will serve as the basis for her MA thesis.

* * *

What I have learned is that every person has pain. Living together here means pain for most of the people. People are in pain because for many of them co-existence has meant that their land has been taken, and they have felt like refugees. For others there is the traumatic memory of the Holocaust, or of brothers or fathers being killed in the wars. There are memories of passing through Arab villages, and having kids throw stones at you. Arab boys and girls have memories of somebody saying nasty things to them.

I have heard so many stories. What is important in a mixed Jewish-Arab group is to listen to that pain, and then try to comfort the person. You simply have to be with them and not say: "Look, you don't have any right to feel this way," or "You shouldn't feel like that because it was just somebody who didn't know any better." If a group knows how to be with people in their sorrow, then it helps, and suddenly there is a change.

Everyone must have the right to be fully human and show all of their colours. Sometimes Jews cannot stand Arabs who criticize Israel. They are tolerant of Jews who speak against the state, but Arabs?... they have no right to speak like that.

After these group experiences the Jewish young people are better able to understand that the Arab young people are very much like them and, more importantly, they understand that even if we do not always agree, it does not mean that we cannot survive together in this same place. It is such a relief when people are able to speak frankly about their fears, hopes, and national feelings because there is something cleansing and freeing about that.

* * *

I was born in Haifa to a mixed family. Both my parents are Jewish, but my father is a Sephardi Jew whose family has been in this place for the last 150 years. My family name was Toledano which means that they originally came from Toledo in Spain.

My mother is from Poland and came here with part of her family in 1933. The rest of the family died in the Holocaust. She was lucky because even in 1933 part of the family realized that things were going to get bad, and so they left.

I grew up and went to school here. My parents taught me that having different traditions does not mean that people cannot get along together, and I know that tolerance has helped me be more open to other people who were different.

My father worked with Arabs, and they used to come to visit us. I think this was possible because Haifa was, and is, a very mixed Jewish-Arab city. I always remember Passover because on the last night some Arab friends would come to eat with us. They brought pita, green onions, yogurt, and olives. All of these things are a part of my Passover memories.

* * *

When I was six years old the 1948 war began. Our home was located just a few metres away from where Arabs and other people were shooting.

I remember running to welcome my father when he came home from work, and everybody was shouting at me because it was an open area and there was shooting. I remember the shooting, but it left no lasting impression on me.

After high school I went to a kibbutz because I was a youth leader in the Hashomer Hatzair movement and thought I should serve society. It took me some time to understand that it is not all the way it sounds because the kibbutz is a place like any other place. The idea that we had in the youth movement was that an academic career was only something for yourself, and since it was an egotistic way to live, I thought I should not go to the university.

After I left the kibbutz, I went to work as a youth leader in a slum area of Haifa, trying to learn how to be a friend to the children there. At that point I didn't necessarily want to help people, but only to learn how to become close to them. I was trying to get to what Martin Buber spoke of as the "I and Thou", being in the other's skin and trying to understand by having a dialogue, not by just teaching. Soon I realized that I lacked the proper skills to do this and needed more training.

What really helped was taking acting lessons from an Israeli actress named Nola Chilton. We became close friends, and from her I learned how to put on another person's skin. In acting one doesn't just imitate, one tries to understand what is going on inside a person by observing its expression in outward behaviour.

I was thirty years old when I finally went to the university to get my first degree in sociology and education. When I finished I went back to work in a youth club, which was trying to develop a group of young leaders from the slum areas of Haifa.

A little later somebody asked me if I would like to have my group meet a group of Arab kids. My partner and I spoke to our group, and they decided to invite the Arab kids to participate in our leadership course. That mixed group worked together for 2½ years, so that means that they really grew up together. I had no experience in doing group work with Jews and Arabs, but just tried to use my intuition and what I had learned from my studies in sociology and education.

We began to create tools to promote a real encounter between Jews and Arabs. The woman who was my partner now lives at Neve Shalom, and for some years she has been the driving power to establish the School of Peace there.

* * *

You may have heard that in Israel the problem is the Oriental Jews, that they are the ones who hate the Arabs. But through our work we discovered that the hatred is simply a shell because Oriental Jews and Arabs are culturally very much alike. Many of the Jews in our group were Orientals, but there were also some of European background. Some were religious and some were not.

Many of the Oriental Jewish kids were ashamed of their culture. For the most part, that is true in Israel. It is really a stigma if you speak Arabic or listen to Arabic music. You are encouraged to be "Western" in your outlook, and to get rid of your culture because supposedly it is primitive and ugly.

This was a lesson the Orientals learned when they came to Israel. Many of the European Jews looked at them and said: "Well, you didn't participate in building Israel, you didn't fight in the wars, so how can you identify with the rest of us Israelis?" As a result, the Orientals tried to prove themselves by hating both the Arabs and their own culture.

We believed that these kinds of ideas were doing a lot of damage to the kids, and it was wonderful to watch them realize that their culture was good and that other people could enjoy it. A number of the Arab kids knew how to play musical instruments, and when they sang it was obvious how proud they were of their culture. We really tried to encourage them to perform often. It was my experience that in such encounters both parties gained something. They enjoyed themselves because it was just plain fun.

I tell you I was surprised how easily it went. I told myself that I was being naive, that it was a dream and there had to be problems that I just wasn't seeing. Some of the Jewish kids thought that something was wrong. "How can we be having such good relationships with Arabs?" they asked. "This is not patriotic, because we are supposed to hate these people."

Jews and Arabs have stereotypes of each other, and the encounters helped kill some of those. For example, the Jewish kids thought that the Arabs were really rich, and had built themselves beautiful villas. The Arab kids thought that the Jews only lived in prestigious neighbourhoods. When they visited each other, they realized that there were some very poor kids on both sides.

The overall experience was good, but in our first effort we were not trying to deal with the deeper problems between Jews and Arabs because we were just beginning our work. Our goal was to train youth leaders capable of dealing with social problems.

I'll tell you what really worried me. In Israel there is a very strong opposition to and fear of marriage between Jews and Arabs. I was afraid that at the age of 15 to 18 romances would begin, and that would have been the end of us. However, nothing happened that we couldn't handle.

* * *

After this first experience my partner and I decided to do something on a larger scale, and we realized that teachers were the population we should try to reach. We worked to develop course models for educators in the high schools, and organized some seminars to formulate a model for Jewish-Arab workshops. Our main goal was to promote a dialogue that would really touch what is important to people. We realized, however, that unless people met each other as human beings first, they would not be able to have a real dialogue. A foundation must be created at the beginning.

First, we try to get to know each other face to face. We use all kinds of games so that the kids can have fun, and at the same time get to know each other in a deeper sense. After that, we begin to work on the stereotypes. We also discovered how important it is that the encounter last more than a day: if the group breaks up after only one day, the kids may be just getting to know each other, and if everything ends too soon they may end up parting like enemies.

All my life I have worked in education, but because I am also a sociologist I doubt that education alone can change the world. However, I can see that it really changes individuals because I have seen that happen. After every workshop I do, I can see changes in people.

* * *

Right now I am working as a research assistant on a project assessing Jewish and Arab attitudes towards each other inside Israel. In addition to the survey of the populations, we are doing a survey of the leadership of both groups.

We used a questionnaire to assess the attitudes of 1,200 Jews and the same number of Arabs. Of these we have chosen 140 Jewish and Arab leaders to interview. These people represent the full political spectrum, and we hope to learn their feelings about mutual co-existence between Jews and Arabs in Israel.

We have the results of the questionnaire and have finished interviewing the leaders. The results are not yet final because there are some adjustments to be made, but I can say that democratic values seem to be very vulnerable in Israel. Twenty-five percent of the Jewish population thinks that Arabs should be prevented from voting in elections. Fifty-seven or 58 percent say that Jews who want a Palestinian state alongside Israel in the West Bank and Gaza should be prevented from voting. Seventy percent say that Israeli Arabs who support such a state should not be allowed to vote.

If you ask Israelis they will say that this is a democratic country, but now you have a considerable portion of the population ready to eliminate the voting rights of both Jews and Arabs. What is encouraging, however, is that only 5 percent said that they would act violently if the government decided to give back the occupied territories. Some said they would strike, but more than 50 percent said they would accept it.

Our research has shown that the Palestinians do not accept Israel as a Zionist state, and they are also not willing to accept a situation where they are second-class citizens. They will fight for their rights, and they feel a great deal of solidarity with their Palestinian brothers and sisters. Two-thirds identify themselves as Palestinians, but in one way or another they also identify themselves with Israel. They don't accept the Zionist character of the country and see Zionism as a racist ideology, but only about 10 percent are not ready to compromise.

They want to see an end of the Law of Return or, if not, a Law of Return instituted for Palestinians as well. Most of all they want equal rights. For example, if you are an Arab, you don't do military service, and many social benefits are only available to army veterans. If you want to study in the high technical institute, aeronautics for example, you are prevented because of security considerations. Some of these restrictions have nothing to do with security, and should be removed if we really want Arabs to live as equals in this society.

We need more than education. I am opposed to violence because it solves nothing. I can go on doing educational and political work, but what is needed is a change in the system.

* * *

People in Israel perceive themselves as democrats, but they really don't try to find out what that means and what kind of commitment they must make in order for democracy to survive here. They don't try to discover what their real obligation is. While most of the country is embarrassed by Kahane's blatant racism, it did make people more aware because before we didn't hear anything about racism and the lack of equal rights.

The experience of Lebanon was terrible, but on the other hand, it helped people draw back the curtain and question our ideas of justice and our feelings about being victims. We Jews feel we are victims even when we are victimizers, but for the first time the Lebanon war made us question our commitment to serve in the army. However, the price for both Palestinians and Israelis was terrible.

* * *

Israel must decide either to end the Israeli-Palestinian conflict or go on oppressing the Palestinian population. By oppressing them, we become the oppressor and that means that we dehumanize ourselves. We cannot allow that, and if we do it it will ruin us.

Israel is not a very good place to live in right now. It is not a secure place, and that is what it was created to be. We Jews must have a refuge, but the Palestinians must have the same. We should understand that because we know what it is like to be refugees.

Israel is also not an attractive place for Jews to come to. People, especially young people, are leaving Israel because it is hard for a young man to grow up knowing that he may be killed in the next war. I have a son and I sometimes think that I have brought him into the world only to be killed. I hope that does not happen, but I feel responsible for Israel and what is going on here.

We have had war after war. People don't have the energy for this any more so they leave. It's our business to solve the Palestinian problem because we suffer from it. Unless we solve it, there will be no peace, and we are paying and will continue to pay a very heavy price for not solving it.

The situation is very complex, and for Jews it has been traumatic. I read the diary of a young man who was killed in the 1967 war. In it he spoke about Yad Vashem, and told his girlfriend that Israel must be strong so that something like the Holocaust does not happen again.

I told you my mother's family was destroyed in the Holocaust. I don't think that it was just by chance that the Holocaust happened. No, it means that Jews have to have their own state. I don't believe that nationalism is the best solution for humanity, but right now we must have a state. I love the people of Israel. Israel is my society; I belong to it, and I want to work for it.

* * *

I don't hate Palestinians because I see that each side fights as though there is no other way. But there is another way, and that is why I work with both Jews and Arabs. I believe that we have to solve the problem together, and we can only do that by being sensitive to each other's problems.

I feel responsible for the society in which I am living, and I have never thought of leaving. Intellectually, maybe I have thought of it, but emotionally — never. I really have to be here. There is no way I can run away; this is my own nation. I feel responsible for what is going on here, and I have to do as much as I can even if I cannot change much.

Martin Buber makes me proud of being a Jew. I remember one of his stories about a rabbi who sees his wife changing clothes and asks where she is going. She says that she is going to court because she is suing her maid. The rabbi says he will accompany her to the court, but she says: "No, I can manage."

"Yes," the rabbi says, "I know you can manage, but what about the poor maid?" This is the part of Judaism that I'm proud of.

Walid Sadik

Walid Sadik, 47, was born in Taibeh, a village near the coastal town of Netanya. An Arab citizen of Israel and a former member of the Knesset, he is politically active and associated with the left-wing Progressive List for Peace Party.

As both a Palestinian and an Israeli citizen, Sadik believes he can more objectively understand both sides of the conflict. "I have studied Jewish culture," he says, "and I have begun to understand more about their motives, but at the same time, I am a pure Palestinian."

In 1983 Sadik was part of an Israeli peace delegation that met with PLO leaders in Budapest. Of that meeting Sadik says: "I was the person who explained Israeli terms to the Palestinians and vice versa. Because of who I am, I was able to help both sides better understand each other."

As the Palestinians see it, they have made a compromise to recognize that Netanya, Jaffa and Ramle are no longer their property. For them this is a compromise and a very generous one. But the Israelis will not give back the occupied territories because they say: "How can we give back what is already ours?" They think that by giving back the West Bank, they are making a sacrifice, but they are forgetting that what they now call Israel was once 85 percent Palestinian.

Why don't we say that this land is a common inheritance and let us partition this inheritance? The Israelis do not want to do that. They want the whole thing, and that won't work. I always say to them: "You have to learn from yourselves. The whole world said that you were not a people, that there was no Jewish people. But you proved that there is a Jewish people even though there was a Holocaust and pogroms and massacres. Finally, you have succeeded. Why can't you let the Palestinians succeed too?"

* * *

Until 1947 I had never personally known a Jew. The only thing I remember is that some of my father's orchards were near the sea, and in order to bring oranges from there, I had to cross a Jewish settlement. The Jewish kids would throw stones at me. We made a game of it, throwing stones back and forth, but that was the only contact I had with them.

Also in 1947 I remember that I knew something was going to happen, but this thing was not exactly clear for me. People said that a war was going to break out between Jews and Arabs because the Jews wanted to expel us from our land and build their own state. We kids rushed through the streets shouting against the Balfour Declaration and the partition, but I did not know who Balfour was or much about the partition.

Then we heard that the Arab armies were coming to help us, and we were very pleased. I remember that I ran about four kilometres to another village in order to read the newspaper telling us about the Arab victories inside Palestine.

On 15 May 1948 I remember the first Arab soldiers from Iraq came and camped in our area. We were very happy to see soldiers — Arab soldiers — coming in order to help and save us. We had heard the terrible stories about Deir Yassin and the massacre there. Because of that we were very frightened of the Jews. Once the muezzin, who called us to prayer, told us that the Jews were coming, all the village fled because they had in their mind the image of Deir Yassin.

We kids went to the Iraqi soldiers and asked them to do something because they didn't seem to be doing much. They told us that they had no orders to fire, and in fact they didn't shoot. They did nothing, but we were supposed to be their servants. I remember I tried to stay away from them because they always asked me to do two things: dig trenches, which they never used, and bring them food. Soon all our high expectations about what they were going to do for us were shattered.

Then suddenly the Iraqi soldiers went back, and the Jordanian army came. They stayed for two weeks in our village, and one day they gathered some of our leaders together and told them that the Jews would come the next day. It was a shock for us and we just couldn't believe it. How could it be that one army arrives and evacuates, and then another army comes only to tell us that the Jews were coming? Where was the pride of the Arab armies?

The next day I was in school and the headmaster looked out the window and said: "Here, they are coming." We rushed to the window and there we saw two jeeps. By this time all the students were crying because we were so afraid.

Half an hour later, the Israelis announced that there would be a gathering in the school yard, and the commander said that from now on we would be under military government. From nine o'clock at night until five o'clock in the morning, there would be a curfew — a permanent one which lasted until 1965. In order to leave the village, we needed a written permit from the military government and this permit was not always given.

The commander also laid down a border and said that none of us should go on the western side of that line. The land on the west side was just taken; my father's groves were there, and we lost the land.

That was a very sad day for me. The day before I had been in the majority, and now I was in the minority. The day before my family had owned land, and in one day it was taken from us. Our economic base of support was completely destroyed because we were part of an agricultural society. A lot of people lost their place of work and their economic resources, but the most humiliating thing was the way the military government treated us. They treated us as slaves, as people not only under occupation, but as people who were not even human beings.

That day was also the first personal interaction I ever had with a Jew, and I remember that the Israeli commander was so rude — savage even. I especially remember his fierce dog which, now and then, he ordered to attack people.

* * *

In 1959 I finished school and applied to study at the Hebrew University. In order to be accepted, I had to get the permission of the military governor, and permission was given. With great hesitation and fear, I went to Jerusalem without any knowledge of Hebrew or of what I was going to do or find there.

That trip from my home to Jerusalem was the first time I travelled in a bus. I was surprised to see the Jewish people because all I had seen before were military people. These Jews surprised me because they did not wear uniforms and they had no fierce dogs. Even after I left the village, every time I saw a Jew I had the image of that commander and his dog.

We were about 22 Arab students at the Hebrew University, and we had our own house because nobody wanted to rent a room to an Arab. After we had been in Jerusalem for a couple months, we heard a knock on the door one night, and saw six Israeli students standing there. They asked if they could come in, and of course as Arabs we knew we had to be hospitable, but we were scared and we said to each other in Arabic: "Here they are, they are the messengers of the military government."

They came in and introduced themselves as being from the Hashomer Hatzair movement and the Mapam Party. They said they had heard about us and wanted to talk to us. They talked about equality and peace with the Palestinians, and how they were against the confiscation of land and the military government. We thought everything they said was just propaganda, but in time we began to investigate the Mapam Party and what lay behind all that they had said to us.

Finally we were convinced that they were really sincere, and that was a turning point for me. I learned that while there were Jews with ugly faces like the military commander, there were others who were rational and cared about us.

Because of those six students, I began to be active in the Mapam Party. Before that I did not dare to think about politics; I thought that if I would be involved, it would endanger my economic situation. At the time the military government wanted us to vote for the ruling party only. I dared to vote for Mapam because, as an Arab, I could find no one to defend me, but with Mapam I had backing in the Jewish state.

* * *

The people of Mapam helped me a lot. From my contact with them, I began to understand why the Jews had come to Palestine. For so many years I had asked: "For God's sake, why did they have to come here?"

Why did the Jews have to come and claim the land? After all, it was land that was not empty; it was not a desert. It was land inhabited by the Palestinian people, and claiming the land was really a crime. I didn't care about the Jews' suffering in Europe because it was not right for them to solve their problems by creating so much suffering for us.

When I got to know Jews, I began to understand how deeply they felt about Palestine and why they felt they were right to have come here. I really began to understand this during my second year at the Hebrew University.

I had moved into the dormitory by then and one day the house-mother told me that there was a group of American students coming to the university, and she wanted me to live with one because she didn't want them all living together. If they did, how would they learn anything about the country? So I said that I would give it a try.

I remember the time I first walked into the room and saw this American. He was an Orthodox Jew from Brooklyn with a beard and kipa. I was shocked. I had expected an American but not this.

When the house-mother told him that he had to live with an Arab, he said: "This is not the reason I came to Israel, to live with an Arab." So she said: "Look, I know this Walid and he is a very good fellow. Try him for three days at least."

Later he told me that I have a very bad habit. I turn over a lot when I am sleeping. During the first three nights, every time I turned in my bed, he thought that I was about to stab him, and he would rush out of the room. That was why he slept with the door open.

You probably won't believe it, but we became great friends during that year. I even learned some Yiddish from him. I turned the lights on and off for him on the Sabbath, and we would go out together in Jerusalem and cry "Shabbas!" (Sabbath) and throw stones at the cars that were passing by and breaking the Sabbath. Because of him I learned to throw stones with a good aim.

I learned the religious connection between Jews and Palestine from him. If you speak to a Jew, he will give you the best claims and arguments in the world to convince you that he has a right to be in this country. Of course, for me, the Palestinians have an even better claim, but what can you do? What can you do if you cannot convince the Jews that their claim is wrong? What can you do if you cannot convince the Palestinians that they are wrong? The fact is you can't do either.

Although I am a citizen of Israel, I am discriminated against because I am also a Palestinian. My land was confiscated, my political liberty was limited, and all the time I am suspect because of my race. But in spite of all these difficulties and obstacles in my way, I know that thinking in realistic terms is better than crying about it all, or stubbornly rejecting possible solutions.

* * *

Up to 1967, the Palestinians had no idea who the Israeli Arabs were, what our status was or what our struggles were. They thought we were all Jews. After the 1967 war, the picture began to be clearer, but at one time we were suspected of being Israeli agents.

The Palestinians had some reason to believe that because, during the days of the military government, the Israelis sent some Arabs to the United States to do propaganda for Israel. They spoke with the Jewish community and the American Congress, and said that Israel was an oasis of democracy which, of course, was not true. After that every Arab who was involved in Israeli politics was viewed as an Israeli agent. Now the situation has improved, and we have good contacts with Palestinian leaders in the West Bank and Gaza. We are also welcomed by the PLO.

It is not easy for me to be a Palestinian and an Israeli citizen at the same time. It is a very great dilemma. I have a double loyalty and what do I do when my state is fighting my own people?

I think as a Palestinian and as an Israeli citizen. I can understand both sides objectively. I have studied Jewish culture and religion, and have begun to understand more about the Jews' motives. But at the same time, I am a pure Palestinian though I was disconnected from them for a period of time. Socially and culturally, I am an integral part of the Palestinian people, but I can understand both sides.

For this reason, I am very active in politics in order to convince people that there are two national movements in this country, but they are like two trains on the same track running towards each other. My task as a Palestinian and as an Israeli citizen is not to hide my identity, but to warn against this collision which is bound to happen unless we can somehow get both trains to stop.

In 1983 I was in Hungary with an Israeli peace group that had been invited by the Hungarian Peace Council. I was the last to enter the hall, and I found the Palestinians sitting on one side of the table and the Israelis on the other side. The dilemma of double loyalty struck me in the face. I asked them where I should sit.

They didn't understand at first, and said that I could choose any place because there were a number of chairs. Then, finally, they realized what I meant. Should I sit with my own people, the Palestinians, or should I sit with my own countrymen? So they said to me: "You will be the chairman of this session", and I sat in between.

For me the session was good. Sometimes I was the person who explained Israeli terms that sounded terrible to the Palestinians, and I also explained to the Israelis some terms which they could not understand. When the Israelis came into the hall, not all of them would shake hands with the Palestinians, but after the six-hour session, they embraced each other. Modestly I say that a lot of this atmosphere was created by me because I was the mediator, and this is the task that I would like to see for Israeli Arabs because we are more objective than either of the other sides.

* * *

Right now the Palestinian state is a very big question mark because even though the Palestinians have succeeded in transforming the issue from a refugee question into a national question, history will judge them on their ability to turn their political ideas into facts. If they can't do that, the alternative is war, and I think that war solves nothing. If war breaks out, the Palestinian people will suffer more than any other people in the region. For this reason, I think that there must be a compromise. The Israelis have to understand that they must restore Palestinian rights and give back the West Bank and Gaza Strip. The Palestinians must be realistic and see things as they are.

I always say to the Israelis that they have to choose between two alternative views of Zionisn. There are those who say that Zionism brought salvation to the Jews by helping them develop their own state so they would be saved from discrimination and oppression in other countries.

I think that Israel, within the Green Line, has provided them this salvation. But if they want the other alternative Zionism which is to bring salvation to the land by building settlements in the West Bank, that will mean a long struggle, with endless wars, and Israel will have to live on its sword.

I ask the Israelis to put themselves in the Palestinians' place. They are dispersed and the whole world is doing nothing more than making speeches and declarations. This desperate situation will push them to do desperate acts. They are not hopeful, and they have not the slightest hint from the Israelis that they are ready to think calmly and rationally.

In this situation the Palestinians have the right to struggle against occupation. All people have this right. But propaganda is against the Palestinians, and they are seen only as terrorists. That is not true, but unfortunately sometimes they do foolish things which strengthen that image.

Sometimes I ask myself why I do this work because it all seems like a closed door. We seem to have no hope, but when I think about the suffering of my people, I know I have to go on even though sometimes I don't even see a ray of hope. Also when I think about those two trains and the collision that may happen, I think that even my modest efforts may be of some use.

Elias Freij

*Mayor **Elias Freij**, 66, of Bethlehem has become one of the most well-known mayors in the world. Outspoken on issues relating to the Israeli occupation of the West Bank, he is deeply concerned about the massive confiscations of land which have taken place since 1967.*

According to Freij, 60 percent of West Bank land has already been lost to Israeli settlements. Before more is lost, he pleads with other Palestinian leaders to accept UN Resolutions 242 and 336 in exchange for Israeli and US recognition of Palestinian rights for self-determination.

"If we lose the land, what will be left for us to talk about?" he asks. "Peace would give us a golden opportunity to prepare the ground for our Palestinian state, but if we lose the land there will come a day when we will regret it and nobody will support us."

I was born in Bethlehem, Palestine, and my family has lived here for centuries. We are part of the Greek Orthodox community. Now most of my family are outside the country. They are living in Brazil, El Salvador, Honduras, the United States and Mexico, because at the beginning of this century Christians began to emigrate from this country.

I was educated in Bethlehem in a British Arabic school during the Mandate, and graduated from high school during the Second World War. Then it was not possible to continue my studies, so I worked during the war here in the family business.

I liked my life very much when I was a child; those days when I was growing up were really good. We had no electricity, no radio, no newspapers, and no cars. It was beautiful. We ate much less meat and depended on lentils and vegetables. We lived very simply here; it was a farmer's life. There was a simplicity and purity of life. You lent people money without a receipt, but they would pay it back. People had some ethics then. Today there are no ethics, and people are more materialistic than they used to be.

* * *

I was one of the few people who accepted the 1947 UN Partition Plan and supported it. I hoped the people would accept some of the British proposals because I was worried. When I was young I had many Jewish friends at school, and I could see how they were organized. I could also see how disorganized we were. We should have accepted the Partition Plan because, considering the circumstances at the time, we could not have expected more. My God, it gave us a lot and by rejecting it we lost a lot, but we can't turn the clock back.

I also remember how Arabic newspapers which were published at that time in Jaffa were telling unrealistic stories. They were deceiving the people and even today some of our newspapers do the same thing. The newspapers were talking about victories over the Zionists and the British — victories which were fabricated out of dreams.

We also had no leadership. There was the Arab Higher Committee, but it was not an organization where people could have a real voice. Most of its permanent leaders were harassed by the British and expelled from the country so they had to send in orders from the outside. What you had was a situation where those on the outside who carried the guns dictated to those on the inside who didn't have guns.

* * *

After partition in 1947, the confrontation began. The British withdrew in May 1948. Either they left behind no Arab authority or they could not establish any. Anyway, everything tumbled on our heads.

Friendships with Jews were cut off after the beginning of 1948. There was so much fighting, and the Jews began to be very, very aggressive. It was dangerous to go into the Jewish quarter in Jerusalem. Then the massacre of Deir Yassin followed in April 1948 when 254 Arab men, women and children were killed. That scared the people.

The people of Bethlehem did not leave because we asked King Abdullah of Transjordan to send us the Arab Legion. They came at the end of 1948, and it was that army which preserved the Arab character of East Jerusalem and of the whole West Bank. Otherwise, the Israelis would have captured all the territory between Jerusalem and the Jordan River. And we, the Palestinians, never gave Jordan credit for that.

The Jordanian army was a small army but an excellent one. Its officers were British so they had to receive orders from London, but they kept the Arab character of this country at a time when no other Arab force on earth could stop the Israelis from taking all of the West Bank. Without the Arab Legion the Israelis would have taken Bethlehem in five minutes.

* * *

Next week we will complete 19 years of Israeli occupation. It has been a bitter, difficult and complex time. It has been a period in which we lost most of our land on which Jewish towns and villages have now been built. And while Arab leaders and Arab kings and Arab politicians — PLO included — talk and argue, Israeli bulldozers are levelling the land. And if we lose the land, what will be left for us to talk about? So far we have lost about 60 percent of the land in the West Bank, and I'm afraid we may have to live with Israeli domination for another twenty years to come. I don't expect any solution in my lifetime, or any solution before the year 2000.

In politics there is no justice, only reality. What is the incentive for Israel to withdraw from all of the occupied territories? I live here, I talk to them; I know them, they know me. I'm not living in Yemen or Damascus. I'm not making hot speeches saying that Israel must withdraw. All right... must, but how? What is to compel Peres, Shamir, Sharon and company to withdraw from Bethlehem and all these beautiful places? Can you tell me? So why do we blind ourselves to the truth?

For Israel, we are the second-best market in the world after the United States. Everything we eat, drink, and use, we get from or through Israel. We pay hundreds of millions of dollars of taxes to Israel, directly and indirectly. In ten years the West Bank will become a Jewish West Bank, and all the Arab slogans in the world are not going to change that.

* * *

Israel has invested billions of dollars on settlements in the West Bank. Here in Bethlehem we are on kilometre 10 from Jerusalem. On kilometre 16 all the land to the right and the left has been taken for settlements. Near

Hebron there is a city called Kyriat Arba. South of Bethlehem they are building a city called Efrat, which is supposed to have 30,000 people and it will have this number within the next few years. Israeli settlers are given full government subsidies for water, electricity, education and taxes. The distance from Efrat to the Hilton Hotel in Jerusalem is less than 20 minutes, so it is very easy to drive to work in Jerusalem where the cost of living is much, much higher. The Israelis are not building today in order to leave tomorrow.

With the Iran-Iraq war exhausting Arabs, with the decline in the price of oil, with Egypt still expelled from the Arab League, with the problems between Iraq and Syria and between the PLO leadership and Jordan, with the relations between Morocco and its neighbours being not so good, and with a man like Gadaffi, tell me, where do we stand? What are the chances that my grandchildren will continue to live in Bethlehem?

Peace would give us a golden opportunity to begin to prepare the ground for our Palestinian state. Without peace we will remain scattered, living as we are in exile and under occupation. And I warn our people that if we lose the land — and we are losing it — there will come a day when we will regret it and nobody will support us.

We should have made peace with Israel in 1948. We should have transformed the truce agreements of 1949 into a peace treaty, and should have realized that Israel is here to stay whether we like it or not. Now Israel, through its superior technology, has become a military super-power. It has a strategic alliance with the United States, and is part and parcel of the United States. The United States will come to defend Israel, so even if the Arabs are able to fight Israel, they will not be able to fight America too. All this about fighting is just nonsense. As long as America exists, Israel will remain strong.

* * *

Kahane? There are about 200,000 Kahanes in Israel, and what scares me is that extremists on the right are growing in number. Geula Cohen started by herself. Now she has a party of three in the Knesset, and politically she isn't much different from Kahane. In any new elections, she and Kahane could end up with five, six or seven seats.

The Jewish young boys hate the Arabs. The Arab young boys hate the Jews. There is a wall of hatred being constructed here and it is frighten-ing. People of my age who lived during the British Mandate had relationships with the Israelis, Jordanians and the British and learned to know them as human beings, but that does not happen much any more.

* * *

I am neither optimistic nor pessimistic. I am a realistic man and I have the courage to express it, not hide it. That makes me feel that I have a duty to serve the people living as they do under occupation. They elected me so I think I am indebted to provide them with all the services they need, and I'm doing that as best as I can.

Israel is in charge of legislation, taxation, security, police, water, land — everything. What do the people have? They have the mayor and they have the council, but in our part of the world all the executive power is in the hands of the mayor.

I built this city hall. I got the money from Abu Dhabi. This building has lifted the morale of the people in Bethlehem. On Saturday, I'm going to open a new well because I want to have an independent source of water for the city, and thank God I got the money for that. I'm going to build two public schools that will be the best in the West Bank. I received the money from Sweden and elsewhere to improve the standard of services in the government hospital here. I'm working with the Knights of Malta to reopen the French hospital that has been closed for two years because of lack of money. I'm really trying to help the people because now survival is the most important thing, and in order to survive they need services.

* * *

Who is endangering Israel's security? Nobody. Some kids throw a stone here or a stone there. They throw a bottle here or a bottle there; out of every ten bottles, one explodes. What the Israelis suffer in road accidents every week is more than what they suffer in a year from stones and bottles. For Israel security is a psychological complex, but what we Palestinians are doing is reinforcing this complex. We are helping the Israelis to be united against us.

The consensus in Europe, America and Canada is that the Palestinians are terrorists. We are not terrorists; we are a peace-loving people. We are people who need peace more than anyone else. We don't want to live under occupation, so we have to wage a campaign of peace. We have to do all we can to stop some crazy Arab boys from committing crimes in Rome, Paris or Vienna.

Europeans are our friends and not our enemies. We should try to build bridges with the United States. The Americans want us to recognize the right of Israel to exist, and I advise the Palestinians to do that and to offer to recognize Israel on a mutual and reciprocal basis. I want the PLO to accept UN Resolutions 242 and 338, providing that the United States will accept our right for self-determination. Then we have to assure the Israeli people — especially Israeli mothers — that we, the Palestinians, need to make peace and live with them as neighbours.

Willy Gafni

Willy Gafni, 55, is project director and one of the founders of the International Centre for Peace in the Middle East, a public policy organization based in Tel Aviv. He has met with most of the Palestinian leadership both in the West Bank and outside Israel, and his pragmatic, realistic viewpoint is respected by Israelis and Palestinians alike.

According to Gafni, the tragedy of the Israeli-Palestinian conflict is that two peoples need the same piece of land. "The Palestinians also need symbols of national pride — a flag and a passport. We should understand", he says, "that they have the same rights as we have to a passport and a national identity."

I lived in Turkey until the age of 11, and came to Israel all by myself — travelled on the train for seven days and crossed three borders. You know, when you think of children today who are 11 years old, you may not even trust them to take the bus from home to school, much less travel alone for seven days.

I remember my mother putting me on the train and waving. We did not know if we would ever meet again. That was during the war in 1942, and there was danger because the Turks were pro-Axis and things were not really clear. The first thing my mother wanted to do was save me, so she sent me to Palestine where I had relatives.

I was born in Istanbul. My parents were born in Germany, but they left before Hitler and came to Istanbul where my father became a professor of German literature at the University of Istanbul.

Maybe this little history is quite important because living in the Middle East when you are young makes you understand better the mentality of the people. From the age of 11 I was brought up in quite an Arabic neighbourhood, and perhaps that may have helped me to understand the situation here better. At any rate, it brought me into contact with Arab people early in my life.

My real contact with Arabs started in 1960. I was a happy bachelor at the time with a huge flat, and I got a phone call from some important person who said: "Willy, we have a problem and we need you to help us out. We have here a friend from Nazareth, an Arab, who has been asked to come three times a week to Tel Aviv to edit an Arab newspaper. And we cannot find a flat for him. The moment people ask his name, the flat becomes unavailable." So he asked, at least until they could find him a flat, would I be able to accommodate him in my place? I said: "Okay, let him come over. I don't know who he is but we'll see."

And there came in a person who, if he had not died ten years ago, could have been one of the best bridges between Arabs and Israelis. His name was Abdul Aziz Zuabi. Later on he was elected to the Knesset and he was the first vice-minister for health — actually the first Arab minister in the Israeli government. He was really a great, great personality — one of the real Arab leaders in Israel and respected by both the Arabs and the Israelis.

I remember my first reaction when he came in. I looked at him and said: "Listen, I don't have a maid here. You are free to feel at home, but if you eat something you had better wash your dishes because I am not going to do that for you."

I think that this attitude of directly putting him on the same level as myself, not trying to be nice to him and not trying to be apologetic or something, was a very, very important point. From my first contact with Arabs, I have always tried to treat them as equals.

After Aziz moved in he never left. Actually, he got married and we lived together, and then I got married and the two couples lived together in the same flat until we found another place. I would say that we were so close that I was like his brother.

The poor guy — you know, he lived in Nazareth and did not have a private car. He used to come to Tel Aviv three times a week by bus and every time he came back from Nazareth he cursed me because his mother forced him to carry a pot of Arabic food for "the Turk". She always called me "the Turk". She knew that I loved stuffed vegetables — leaves and what not — and she used to tell him: "This is for the Turk and you had better take it to him." He hated to go with this pot on the bus from Nazareth to Tel Aviv.

Later on, I managed to hire a maid who came in to clean the house once a week. She was a woman who was born in Tiberias, a third or fourth generation Israeli from the real Sephardi Jews, and she was a character. Aziz also used to bring jars of white, cream cheese balls in olive oil. This is something delicious.

One day Aziz comes home and he finds this woman sitting at the table and eating this cheese. Aziz could not hurt anybody and he did not want to embarrass her, so he said: "I hope you are enjoying the cheese." So she said to him: "Ah, those bastards ... those Arabs, they really know how to make good cheese." Then she looked at him and said: "Wait a minute. Where are you from?" Later he told me: "I did not want to embarrass her, so I told her that I was from Afula", which is a Jewish town near Nazareth.

* * *

From Aziz I learned a lot about the Arabs. I remember that in 1967, after the occupation of the West Bank began, he came to me very excited and said that he had met an old friend of his from grammar school who was now the vice-mayor of Ramallah. Aziz said that he had had long talks with him and that he was very sad and depressed and did not believe that any solution could be reached. He believed that all Israelis were the same even though Aziz tried to explain that Israel has many faces and many different minds and that there were Israelis who could be partners for a dialogue. Aziz asked if I would be ready to meet this man.

By the time we were able to arrange a meeting, the vice-mayor had already been expelled from Ramallah to Jericho. I went down to Jericho and I remember that it was a very, very hot day. He was sitting in a shabby hotel where he had been living since he had been expelled. This was a person who had been quite wealthy, who had had a big villa in Ramallah. Aziz introduced us and said: "Okay, start talking."

I must confess that it was terrible at the beginning. For the first half-hour it was a dialogue between the mute and the deaf. He was citing his slogans, I was citing mine. We couldn't find any beginning of communication between us. It was terrible and I was so frustrated because I had really come to speak to a Palestinian leader. This was something new for me, coming only three months after the beginning of the occupation. Finally, in frustration, I said: "Look, can't we talk like equals?"

His response was: "But we are not equals. I am lying on the floor and you are standing with your foot on my neck and telling me, from the height of 1 metre 75, that we should talk like equals. We are not equals. You are the conqueror and I am the conquered."

This was quite a shock for me because I think that only then did I start to understand that it is not enough to feel or want to feel that the Arabs are equals. The situation is not equal, and therefore we are not equals and you cannot talk to each other as equals.

Only after he said that to me did we really start to talk to each other. We sat for almost five hours and I think that he was one of the most remarkable Palestinian leaders that I have ever met in my life. I think that many of my strong beliefs today are a result of this meeting.

It is interesting that while Aziz was an Israeli Arab and even though he was a strong personality, he could not express the real feelings of the Palestinians like the Palestinians themselves.

Later on, this man was expelled from Jericho to Jordan. During the last 19 years I have tried to meet with him but without success. Recently, I heard that he is the chairman of the bar in Jordan. He has quit politics and is not involved any more. But when he first went to Jordan he was one of the aides to Arafat.

I learned a very important thing from him: the Israelis had won the war of 1967 too easily and too quickly. He said that we Israelis could not understand the suffering of the Palestinians because we did not suffer enough in the war. It was a Blitzkrieg. It was too easy for us; we had not had enough casualties to grasp the tragedy of the war, and therefore it would be impossible to come to an understanding between the two peoples without having another war.

Then he said something quite important that I am now trying to get the Israelis to understand. "You should understand that the Arabs are a fatalistic people. For us time has no value. You have won this war; we lost it. We cannot accept this loss because we cannot accept the shame. We will initiate another war, not because we think we will win it, but because it is in our nature. You will win again and you will take probably a little bit more territory. We will be frustrated and feel shamed again, and we will initiate another war which you will win."

He said that this would happen five, ten, fifteen — I don't know how many times. "But watch it," he said, "you cannot afford to lose one war because that will be the end of you. I don't know how, but let's try to find a way to stop this cycle of wars because at the end of it, you are going to lose."

* * *

The Jews have chosen to live in this part of the world and I think rightfully so because, for a people who have for over 2000 years prayed every year "Next year in Jerusalem", there probably is some kind of right to this part of the world. But without peace, I'm afraid it is only a matter of time before we Israelis become what I call "a historical episode of the Third Temple". That is why peace is so important.

On the other hand, the Palestinian people also have rights to this land. There is only one way out and that is partition. But if the Israelis — and I mean we — will not understand that we have to stop this cycle of hatred, that we have to give the Palestinians something that will make them feel better so they can get out of the cycle of losing face all the time and always having to take revenge, it will only be a matter of time before a catastrophe.

The Palestinians need those symbols that give everyone national pride: a flag and a passport. We should understand that they have at least the same rights as we to have a passport and an identity.

It's not only Israel that is to be blamed for this impasse. The tragedy here is that both stubborn people are not yet ready to grant the same rights to the other side. The Israelis must understand that the Palestinians have rights and the Palestinians must understand that the Jews have no alternative other than living here, and because of that we must have rights too.

* * *

I think that the education Israelis got until 1967, and especially before independence in 1948, was an education marked by high morality. I still remember that in the Haganah and later on in the begininng of the army of Israel, to learn how to use the rifle technically took about three hours. You can teach a soldier how to use a rifle in that amount of time. But in the Israeli army, and before that in the Haganah, teaching *when* to use a rifle took about twenty hours because the emphasis was not on the technical aspect but on the morality of using the rifle. Against whom do you use the rifle? When do you use the rifle?

The moral aspects were very, very demanding and high at that time. You dealt with an enemy; your enemy was a human being. I believe that in the youth organizations and in the army, one of the things that was made very clear to us was that sooner or later we would have to live with the Arabs. This is not an enemy that we will have for ever. Today we have a quarrel about land; we have a political quarrel. But we don't want their land; we don't want to rule the Arabs. We are the victims of the Holocaust. We want a small place here in the Middle East to live, recognizing that the Arabs also have rights. Somewhere along the line we will have to come to some kind of an understanding.

The Israel of Ben-Gurion, Israel before 1967, was a small country and was ready to be a small country if it was accepted by the Arabs who were surrounding it. Unfortunately, the war of 1967 changed a lot of things. Suddenly, this small, moral people who could have been happy staying in small Israel, becomes the conqueror with large conquered territories. There is a kind of drunkenness of victory — easy victory — and it is like easy money: easy come... easy go. Suddenly these young, energetic people began to be very satisfied with themselves. Making money started to be the big aim in life. Everyone wanted fancy cars and to travel around. Suddenly it is a different Israel.

And believe me, it does not help to be a liberal conqueror. A conqueror remains a conqueror. It is not you who decide the norms of your conquest or your behaviour towards the conquered, it is the conquered. The moment they oppose you, you have to retaliate, you have to react and you are not any more the master of your own decisions. The conquered make you act and here is where you begin the escalation. You start with good intentions of being a very liberal conqueror and you find yourself at the end being a conqueror like any other bloody conqueror in the history of the world. You are not any more the master of your own decisions or your own morality.

* * *

I have a lot of criticism about Israel, but I have no less criticism about the Palestinians. Every once in a while, when I'm really frustrated, I say to my Palestinian friends: "To hell with you, why don't you do something for your own selves? Why do you expect us to do it for you?" They expect that we, the Israeli moderates, should do something. It is interesting that in 1962 when I first met Aziz Zuabi, it was a gut feeling, a natural reaction, to tell him: "If you eat something, you'd better wash your own dishes." Now, politically, I tell Palestinians that I'm not ready to do everything for them; I'm not a Jew who has a bad conscience or something, who has to do something for the poor guys, the Palestinians. I tell them: "You do for yourself, and I'll help you."

The Palestinians have, like I have, two kinds of problems. The first is to change public opinion. Instead of the politicians being dragged by public opinion, they should lead it. But politicians are cowards all over the world. They will follow the camp, not lead it. There are some politicians who have led, but they are not politicians. They were leaders and statesmen like Churchill, De Gaulle, Roosevelt. Unfortunately, in the Middle East we don't have a De Gaulle or a Churchill. We don't have any leader — real leader — who could say: "I can promise you tears and blood and sweat." So it is the task of people like me, who are not leaders and not politicians, to try and influence public opinion, to try to make people understand that the problems in this area are such that if we don't deal with them today, like cancer, it will be too late to deal with them later.

Secondly, we have to educate generations — on both sides — that it is our destiny to live together in this part of the world and both peoples have to choose whether they are going to live in a series of wars or not. I always tell the Palestinians: "Don't you kid yourself, with modern technology we are going to destroy each other. There will be no victory."

If we want to avoid the tragedy — for both peoples, for the other people in the region and maybe the whole world — we had better find a solution. It is our task — and this is what I demand from the Palestinians too — to be more courageous, to stand up and say our minds, even though I recognize the big difference between me, as an Israeli moderate, and the Palestinian moderate. He may risk his life; I risk a professional position... maybe. But people like Issam Sartawi, they have really risked and paid with their lives.

* * *

The truth, the bare truth, is that somewhere the key to this problem is in the hands of the Israelis. The Israelis have to understand that, unfortunately for both sides, the Palestinians do not have a strong leadership — strong enough to lead their people towards a change in attitude and behaviour.

Israel, in its behaviour towards the Palestinians, could strengthen the leadership. If you want to strengthen the leadership of your opponent, you have to give them something. If you give your opponents something, they can have more courage; they can have more leeway to change attitudes and to change policies.

In other words, if it is true that Arafat is still the leader of the Palestinians, we can influence whether he will be a strong leader who can make concessions or a weak leader who can never make concessions. So it is our choice to decide whether we want a strong Arafat or a weak Arafat. Now with a strong Arafat I can deal, because only a strong Arafat can deliver the goods. With a weak leader I'd better not deal, because anything he promises me won't be kept anyway, so what's the point of giving him anything? This is the Israeli choice.

On the other hand — and this is what I always call the tragic parallel — Arafat and his company should understand that public opinion in a democratic society like Israel has a lot of influence on policy-makers. The way the Palestinians have chosen — what they call the "armed struggle" and we and most of the rest of the world call "terror" — is actually against their best interests.

Instead of creating Israeli pressure to give the Palestinians what they want, they are getting exactly the opposite. They are getting a strong, angry Israel that says: "With those bastards — those killers of women, children and old men — we don't want to deal." The fact is that the Palestinians have to stop terror. Only then can an Israeli leader or politician offer something to Arafat that is worthwhile so that he can change Palestinian attitudes and be the leader he should be.

* * *

What I demand from the Palestinians is not the recognition of Israel, which for them is still too difficult, but a cease-fire for a period of time — one year, half a year, one-and-a-half years — with the understanding that this decision to stop the armed struggle is a sign of goodwill from the Palestinian side. The Israelis would then recognize the Palestinians as a partner in negotiations.

We have this great task to work on confidence-building because it is true, like Sadat said, that the problem is 70 percent psychological. My first meeting with Issam Sartawi was seven or eight hours of difficult, political talk. Four or five months later, when we met again in Paris, he hugged me like a long-lost brother. It surprised me a little because, you know, we were still two enemies meeting. And I told him so.

Then he said a very interesting thing: "Willy, what impressed me very much in our first meeting was that you said that we were meeting as enemies, that you represented your own people and I represented mine. Let's now try and see if we can come to some kind of solution without shouting at each other. But let us not forget that we are enemies."

* * *

Israeli fears... here the psychological element is very, very strong. It is strange actually. Average Israelis have no problem when it comes to a war with the Arab world. They know that we are going to win the war. All the Arab countries against us, including Russia? No problem; there will be a victory. But when it comes to the Palestinians in our own backyard in the West Bank, they have fears. They have apprehensions and you can't explain it.

Sometimes I ask Israelis: "What are you talking about? The Syrian army... the Egyptian army... the Jordanian army... Iraq — with these you don't have a problem, but with one-and-a-half million Palestinians in your backyard here you are scared to death. Why?" No answer.

My feeling is that there is a difference between military fighting and terror fighting. In terror fighting, you fight ghosts and it is normal for humankind to be afraid of ghosts. Ghosts you can't visualize. In a war there is a front and on one side you've got a division. On the other side you've got a division too, and you have tanks and airplanes and you see the enemy, so you fight.

With terror, you are fighting ghosts. To add to that, the Palestinians continue, unfortunately, to speak about the destruction of Israel. That means that not only are you fighting a ghost, but a ghost that is declaring that it wants to destroy you. So you start to hit in all directions. To deal with fears of this kind is very, very difficult.

This is why I emphasize that it is the duty of the Palestinians to declare a cease-fire in order to let Israeli emotions rest a little bit. Then we will be able to understand that we are no longer dealing with a ghost, but with a political problem. There is Arafat, there is his executive committee; they are real, not ghosts.

In 1978, at the same time as Camp David, the International Centre for Peace in the Middle East had a conference at the American Colony Hotel in Jerusalem. It was called the "Mini Camp David". A very interesting thing happened there. One of our leading writers, Amos Oz, participated along with a very extremist Palestinian leader from Gaza. And Oz concentrated exactly on this inexplicable Israeli fear of the Palestinians. He said to this Palestinian: "You'd better believe me that it is not an excuse. We really, sincerely are afraid."

It was the first time that this Palestinian had heard the fear expressed in this way, and he stood up and said: "You know what? I believe it. I really think that you Israelis have a problem and therefore we Palestinians have a problem, because we don't understand that you really, sincerely are afraid. We thought until now that it was propaganda, that it was a kind of excuse. So we have to deal with it; we have to understand it."

* * *

Palestinians want Israel to recognize their right for self-determination. This is one thing. The second thing is more concrete: they want us to accept a few of the Palestinian leaders from the mainstream of the PLO leadership — from Fatah — to take part in the Jordanian-Palestinian negotiations. That's all. I see no reason why this is impossible.

From there the way is still very long but this should be the first step. This willingness to deal with the PLO's leadership should be in return for the Palestinian declaration that they will stop the terror for a certain period of time and recognize that the state of Israel exists. This is really a foolish thing because Israel already exists, but it should show at least that they are ready to repudiate this thinking that they want to destroy Israel. If they want from us the acknowledgment of their right for self-determination, then they must recognize our right to existence as well.

Does Arafat have the power to stop the terror? I'm not so sure. He had it once but I'm not so sure if he has it any more. I would say, however, that right now he is the Palestinians' only leader because they don't have anybody else. But if the situation continues as it is for another year or two, one of two things may happen: he will either vanish as a leader or he will go back to the rejectionist camp. One of his arguments against his dissidents — against Abu Musa and so on — is that Israel cannot be destroyed, that the Palestinians have to come to terms with Israel on a political level. The PLO extremists say to him: "You are fooling yourself; you won't get anything from Israel."

So this is what I said before. The Israelis can either strengthen or weaken Arafat. An Arafat that gets nothing from the political process will have to revert to military means and this means terror.

There is a difference between Arafat and Sadat: Sadat was an enemy, but Arafat is a ghost and that is why it is easier to demonize Arafat. When Begin said about Arafat: "This is an animal on two legs", it was accepted by the Israelis. This was part of the demonization of the PLO and with a demon, you don't talk — with a ghost, you don't talk. Arafat is one day here, one day there, one day this, one day that... who is it? Abu Nidal, Abu Musa... you don't even know with whom to deal here.

And let us not forget that the feeling in Israel for annexing the occupied territories is getting stronger and stronger. As one of the important leaders in Israel once told me: "Are you crazy? Should we negotiate with the Palestinians? What does it mean to negotiate. In negotiations you give and you take, but I don't want to give anything."

So it is done on purpose — this demonization of the Palestinians — and therefore a situation is created where it seems that since there is nobody to talk to, you don't have to talk. You don't have to give anything, because you are not negotiating.

* * *

I believe what we have here is a kind of Greek tragedy. Both peoples are marching with drums towards their tragic end, and you feel that there must be somebody to cry in the wilderness and try and stop them from this terrible destiny. I know that I am living and want to continue living in the Middle East. I have no other choice. Both peoples have no other choice. We either have to live together, or we will destroy each other and pull down the whole house like Samson.

Ora Namir

Ora Namir was born 55 years ago in the northern coastal town of Hadera. At the age of six she moved with her parents to a moshav near there. After college she joined the Israeli army and served during the 1948 independence war.

For the past 14 years Namir has been a member of the Israeli Knesset, and currently serves as chairperson of the Labour and Social Welfare Committee. The Lebanon war and the country's shift to the political right — especially among young Israelis — prompted her to become more involved in peace activities, and she is now recognized as one of the most outspoken peace activists in the Labour Party.

Namir believes that peace will not be achieved until violence ceases. "When I talk to Israelis about trusting the Arabs," she says, "the first thing I say to them is that if wars will continue, there will be less and less trust. Only if wars stop will we have trust. If we want wars to stop, we must sit down and talk to each other."

My parents never taught me to hate the Arabs. I did not feel any atmosphere of hatred towards them either in my home or at school — nowhere where I was brought up.

My parents played a great role in my life. When I talk about peace, always I quote my parents. I quote what I received at home. Why did they come as pioneers to this country? What was the motivation?

Parts of my father's family and my late mother's family went to the United States — pursuing the "American Dream". But my parents chose to come to Palestine and they had two reasons: first to form a Jewish state — a Jewish state, not half Jewish and half non-Jewish. The second reason was to form a state based on the values of the Jewish faith. These values include the belief that the human being is the centre of society. Also, the human being is not only a Jew but is first of all a human being, regardless of his or her religion, nationality and beliefs. The Jewish faith is based on respect among human beings and equality, on helping the weak in the society and respecting minorities. These, if you ask me, are my beliefs and I received them only from my parents.

I don't have to be an Orthodox Jew to believe in these human values. When people say: "Well, we thought that in Israel everyone is very Orthodox", I say: "No, the very fact that I live in Israel is a very Jewish fact."

What is it to be Jewish? Do I have to go to a synagogue for that? I mean, the whole religious issue for Jews in this country is very complicated because in Israel today the great majority of the population is non-Orthodox. We call many of these people "traditional Jews", but I would think that at least half of the Jewish population, if not more, are not even traditional Jews.

We have religious parties that receive maybe 11 percent of the vote in elections, and since we have so many political parties the government is always formed by coalitions. So what you have is a small religious minority holding a power balance in any government. It is a power well in excess of the actual number of Orthodox Jews in this country, so it is an unrepresentational power.

The religious parties know very well how to make the most of this power. More than any political party they know how to play it, and they have always vetoed having in Israel Conservative and Reform synagogues. Until now, unfortunately, they have been very successful so if you come to Israel today you will see either very Orthodox or non-Orthodox — what we call non-religious Jews.

* * *

We have today within our country half a million Arabs who are citizens of the state of Israel, and as such are equal by law. In the occupied territories we have more than one-and-a-half million Palestinians, which means that if we annex the territories to the state of Israel, we shall have a population within our borders of about two million Arabs. There are about three and a half million Jewish citizens in Israel. Demographically speaking, in no time and without any wars, it is obvious that this will not be any more a Jewish state. Therefore, from a Jewish point of view, Israel will not be a Jewish state, and if it is no more a Jewish state, why should we live here? Why shouldn't we live anywhere else in the world?

The second point is that if we do not annex the territories but continue to occupy them, the Arabs there will not be citizens and will have no rights. However, if we do annex, most Israelis will not want the Arabs to become citizens because that means that one and a half million more Arabs will have the right to vote. If they have the right to vote, they will have a very large representation within our Knesset and will become very influential. Again, all of this would happen without wars. So, of course, these people who want to annex the territories do not want to give the Arabs any rights.

I think that only a very small minority in this country believe that the Arabs can be thrown out. Whether we like it or not, the Arabs see this country as their home. They do not volunteer to leave and live somewhere else. So we are developing into a country where parts of our population — and to my regret these are large parts of the population — are not so keen either on equality or human rights when we discuss the status of the Arabs in the territories.

What has happened in Israel since the founding of the state makes it out to be a very different country from what it was intended to be. The principles it was founded upon have been changed. I must say that I have a lot of difficulty living in such a country.

* * *

When my parents went to live on the moshav in 1937, there were terrible fights with the Arabs, and the area where we lived was in the middle of these events. There was a lot of shooting and killing during the nights. I remember it very well. We used to gather all of the families together to defend ourselves and to protect children and elderly people, and the men used to keep guard. But I also remember that I never developed any kind of hatred towards the Arabs — never.

When I was young, I had very few opportunities to meet Arabs at all. I think the first Arabs that I really met were those in the Knesset. I have been in the Knesset for the last 14 years, but I had worked there some years back. At that time I knew the Arab members, and I really had no reason to hate them.

When I was first elected to the Knesset I was active in the education committee and later on I became the chairperson. During that time I was very disturbed by the fact that the educational system in the Arab villages and towns in Israel was so neglected. I devoted a lot of my time to contribute something to improve the standard and the government's policy towards the schools. Again, you know, it is so difficult because of the Israeli complex that all the Arabs are our enemies. It is a very complicated situation for an Israeli as long as the wars continue.

* * *

I feel understood by the Arabs. I have no problem to communicate with them. This is, in my opinion, the issue: to some Israelis — and I hope they are a real minority — Arabs are not human beings. This is because of the wars, because of the atmosphere around the wars, and because of the fact that almost every Israeli is serving in the army. For them the Arabs are their enemies, and you know wars and humanity do not go together — it just doesn't work.

The other people — a larger number of Israelis — do not believe that you can trust the Arabs. That is why they do not believe in negotiations. That's why I believe — and I am very convinced about this — that the minute we can sit together, we can freely and openly discuss issues. We can tell them to their face what we don't like, what we don't believe in. They can say the same to us, but I'm sure that there will be many, many issues that we can settle. The first step, which is so very difficult, is to convince the Israelis to have some kind of a trust in the Arabs. This is the hardest part of it.

When I talk to Israelis about trusting Arabs, the first thing I say to them is that if wars continue, there will be less and less trust. If we want wars to stop, we must sit together, but I am not that naive: I do not believe that without the involvement of the two big powers we will be able to sit together. It is not only a question of me and some of the Palestinians in the West Bank; involved in it are other Arab countries, other Arab leaders, with other motivations. It's not only peace between Israel and the Arab world, it is the Palestinian problem, forming another state — where, how, in what connection?

* * *

There is a very real fear in Israel about security. How do we defend ourselves if something happens? You know our history worries us very much. We are small and unfortunately not many Jews come to live here. It's not only a question of hating the Arabs, it's very, very involved, and the hardest dispute is among the Jewish community in this country. I think it is even harder than between people like myself and the Arabs.

I take Gush Emunim for example. You know, they are great believers in what they are doing. They are believers; they are pioneers. The arguments among us — the Jewish people — are very, very profound arguments. We share the same fate and belief. We want a Jewish state, but the question is how do we secure our state? The Gush believe in not giving away anything to the Arabs, in being very hard with them on negotiations. For us, if I speak about the peace process, this is the barrier, not the Arabs. There is now in this country no national agreement on the issue of peace. We all say that we want peace, but we are very different and very far away from each other on how to reach it, and what we are willing to pay for it.

* * *

In the past years there have been two turning points for me. The first one was while I was on the education committee, and I met many of the younger people who tended towards the political right. They had a very strong nationalist attitude and they were less and less sensitive towards what I call justice, humanity, and respect for each other. There was a growing belief in physical strength. This is one thing that worried me very much, and I came to the conclusion that education in a vacuum is not influential.

The second thing was the war in Lebanon. I started to get very, very afraid that governments — and I say *governments* in Israel — can use our army, that was formed for defence and was kept as such, to solve political problems or change attitudes.

These were the two incidents that made me become more active on political issues. Until then I devoted most of my time to education. But I came to the conclusion that education alone will not change the situation. If we don't change the atmosphere, if we won't change the situation, education will not be influential at all. We change the atmosphere by making peace.

First of all, only a first-row politician can initiate a change in atmosphere, and in this government no one can do it. On this issue a government can fall in Israel. If you don't have the majority of the people behind you, it is very difficult, and neither of the large parties in Israel has a majority.

* * *

I believe in what I do. I believe in my work which is trying to better the life of the people in my own country — especially the life of the weak in society. Second, I do believe that we will reach peace. There is no alternative — no other way. No one can assure us that in all the wars we shall always be the winner. We have had one war that we almost lost —

the Yom Kippur War. I hope that the world will not wait until another war starts because this will be dangerous not only for Israel or the Middle East, but for the whole world. You know what kind of arms are used today.

I hope that in the near future the main powers will come to the conclusion that they must be involved, and then it will be easier for us to make peace. If there is no possibility for peace, it will mean a different state of Israel because it will have a different character. It will mean very different values. If that happens, people like me will have no reason to live here.

I want to see an Israel existing on the same foundations upon which it was based — on the values, elements, and foundation of the Jewish faith. For that, we need peace. Without peace, without coming to some understanding with the Arabs, it won't happen.

Zuheir Rayyes

Zuheir Rayyes *is a lawyer, journalist, and chairman of the Arab Council for Public Affairs in East Jerusalem. The Council's activities range from book publishing to the development of appropriate technology. Of special interest to the Council is preserving Palestinian culture thereby providing Palestinians with a historical link to their past.*

The 53-year old Rayyes was one of the founders of the Palestine Liberation Organization, and participated in drafting its charter. Regarded as an influential Palestinian leader, Rayyes has participated in numerous meetings with international diplomats visiting the area.

While understanding the Israeli need for security, Rayyes says that all parties must have the political courage to push beyond their fears. "Peace", he says, "can only be achieved by negotiation."

I was born in Nazareth, but went to school in Gaza. When the 1948 war began, I went to Egypt to finish two secondary grades, and later I was accepted into the faculty of law at Cairo University. I received my law degree in 1954. I don't practise law any more, but do work as a legal consultant and recently helped establish the Gaza Centre for Law and Rights, a non-profit centre interested in research and defending human rights.

All of my life I have tried to be of some help to the local people here. After the Israeli occupation began I helped establish the Union of Citrus Growers and then worked to organize the first cooperative for citrus marketing. Together we built a $1 million citrus packaging house by selling shares to the public.

* * *

As any other child in a society such as ours, I was influenced by my parents and other members of the family. Our tradition is one of the consolidated family, so we children always see our elders as ideals and we try to follow in their footsteps.

My father was an educator. He was the general director of education in the Gaza Strip, and before that in the southern district of Palestine. His work was especially important after 1948 when we had no schools here. I still remember the tents where the students sat on cement blocks, and the teachers were paid for teaching with food rations. My father organized these schools, and his effort in this field was recognized by UNESCO.

My first experience with Israelis was during what we call the Tri-partite Aggression into Sinai in 1956. I was arrested at that time and was freed only after the Israeli withdrawal. I remember in the first days of the 1967 occupation, all of us were expecting to be killed by the Israelis, but as a matter of fact although this occupation is something unbearable and very hard, we prefer the Israelis to the Egyptians who occupied Gaza before.

For months and months after the occupation, we had to ask for a permit to go to Nazareth or Jerusalem. As time passed we began to realize that there were two kinds of Israelis: one was the military represented by the governor general and the occupation authority, and the others were human beings like the Israelis who live in Tel Aviv and Jerusalem.

We began to make some connections with the Israelis, and to exchange views. As a result we realized that there is the common human element after all; they are human like we are. When we began our political struggle, we found that there were many Israeli intellectuals and others who supported us.

This fact encouraged us to have more encounters, and relationships developed which helped create the understanding that mutual recognition should take place. The Palestinians want their human rights and self-determination, but we also believe that if you want your freedom, it should not be at the expense of others' freedom. If you want self-determination, you shouldn't deprive others of their rights. It is simply logical and something that corresponds to common-sense.

* * *

In my meetings with understanding Israelis, I really feel that they are honest. Furthermore, I feel that even some of the military people understand, but they simply have to obey orders.

Once an Israeli military man asked me what I thought about the invasion of Lebanon. I told him that I felt occupying land was dangerous because it would turn the Israeli people into conquerors of the Arab population. I said that military force was not the way towards peace, and this man said: "I totally agree with you, and those who agree with 'Raful' (Rafael Eitan, the then Israeli chief of staff) are only 5 percent of the Israeli army."

After that he came to visit me and brought greetings on the occasion of the Muslim feast. You know, every time you visit someone for the feast, you just spend five or ten minutes at the most, but he spent two hours just because we had something to discuss, and I think he enjoyed expressing his feelings. I was sure that the man was in a position that obliged him to do his duty, and that was why he could not act on his own convictions.

From my point of view even some of the Israeli extremists understand, but do not want to face the fact that they have to make concessions and give us something as a price for peace. They have not yet convinced themselves that they have to pay this price, and are waiting for us to succumb to their expansionist ideas.

* * *

I understand the Israeli need for security, but this does not, in any way, justify what they do to make themselves feel secure. I cannot ask them to leave the occupied territories now without any preparations or guarantees for their own security, but that does not justify the continuation of the occupation.

We Palestinians, too, have security problems, but I hope that a reasonable solution can be found. I know one thing, however, and that is that I don't want the Israeli's "national security rope" to strangle every effort for a lasting and solid peace.

The question is how to go beyond the fears. I feel that peace can only be achieved by negotiation. Now the Israelis are tiring us and themselves by pushing to create an alternative leadership in the West Bank. They are stubbornly trying to avoid negotiations with the PLO when the PLO is the only adequate body which can logically and reasonably sit at the negotiating table with them. Any other group has no legitimacy in the eyes of the Palestinians. Negotiating with others would just side-step the problem.

It is the same as the Israeli experiments to establish what they called the "Village Leagues". This was nonsense because nobody would have anything to do with these leagues because they did not represent the

Palestinian people; they were just forced on us by the Israelis. Finally, they fell apart without even as much as a good-bye from the Israelis.

I'd really like to see the revival of the Palestinian-Jordanian agreement, and after that the movement towards negotiations for peace through a joint Jordanian-Palestinian delegation. Second, I'd like to see some sort of declaration of intentions from the Israelis which would lead to the recognition of Palestinian self-determination. Of course this eventually would mean that we would have our independent state.

Deep down I think the Israelis understand this situation very well, but they are avoiding reality in the hope that the problem will just go away, and then they can have all of the land. All the time we try to convince the Israelis that if they really want peace, they have our address — they know where we are.

* * *

You asked me if I ever get discouraged. You know, sometimes I just don't get out of bed; I stay there for a few days because things seem so discouraging. But I feel it is my duty to keep struggling, to persist and remain steadfast. It is part of my commitment to myself, my family, my people, and my nation — that's it. Sometimes I am not happy with this, but nevertheless it is my duty to continue because I have no choice.

I do always try to be optimistic; there is no choice but to be optimistic. Kahane's and Sharon's idea of pushing all of the Palestinians out is impossible. So is trying to keep us without passports and without law.

If the Israelis formally annex Gaza and the West Bank and don't give political rights to the inhabitants, they will face a situation not unlike the one now in South Africa, and it will be hell for them. The other alternative is to give us citizenship and full rights which will mean the political end of the state of Israel as a uniquely Jewish state. I see that there is no other way than recognizing the rights of the Palestinians for self-determination, and allowing us to establish our own independent state alongside Israel.

* * *

Kahane doesn't make me feel anything because I think he is just an alibi for every Israeli extremist with civilized features. I think it's easy for Israelis to put all the blame on Kahane while they themselves should be blamed more than Kahane — at least he says what he is thinking. Now that Kahane is here, Israelis are happy that there is someone they can point to and say: "Don't look at me, look at him."

I hope the Americans, especially, will be able to see the Palestinians through clearer eyes because in the United States public opinion affects the government's policy. As Palestinians we do not have the means to go to the United States and explain everything. There have been instances of tragedy, for example in Lebanon, when the United States' administration did not act well, and the American public was not given the whole picture.

I fear that power will continue to be in the hands of unreasonable parties, and that things will continue to deteriorate — as we see in Lebanon where everything has been demolished, and the rule of the jungle is in force. The reasonable people of the world must unite and stand together or else there will be a great tragedy.

Glossary

Aliyah: "Ascent": Jewish immigration to Israel.

Aliyah Bet: Illegal Jewish immigration to Palestine in defiance of British restrictions (1934-1948).

Balfour Declaration: British declaration (1917) of support for a Jewish home-land in Israel. "His Majesty's Government view with favour the estab-lishment in Palestine of a national home for the Jewish people, and will use their best endeavours to facilitate the achievement of this objective, it being clearly understood that nothing should be done which may prejudice the civil and religious rights of existing non-Jewish communities in Palestine..."

Begin, Menachem: Israeli Prime Minister (1977-83) and commander of the Irgun. Best known for uncompromising stand on retaining the territories captured in 1967 war.

Ben-Gurion, David: Israel's first prime minister.

Black September: The 1970 eviction of the Palestine Liberation Organization (PLO) from Jordan.

British Mandate: League of Nations' authority for British rule of Palestine (1920-1948).

Chanuka: Feast of Dedication. An eight-day Jewish festival instituted by Judah Maccabee to commemorate his purifying the Temple in Jerusalem.

Cohen, Geula: Member of the Knesset and the right-wing Tehiya Party.

Deir Yassin: Arab village near Jerusalem where in April 1948 the Irgun (under the command of Menachem Begin) massacred 254 Arab civilians.

Diaspora: The Jewish community living outside Israel.

Fez Plan: Also known as the "Fahd Plan" (for Crown Prince Fahd of Saudi Arabia). Gave *de facto* recognition to the state of Israel by stating that all countries in the region have the right to live in peace. Adopted at the 1982 Arab summit meeting at Fez.

Greater Israel: Refers to the religious-nationalist belief that ancient Israel contained territory in what is now Jordan, Syria and Lebanon.

Green Line: Israel's pre-1967 war borders.

Gush Emunim: "The Block of the Faithful": religious-nationalist group whose aim is to place civilian settlements in the occupied West Bank.

Haganah: "Defence": the pre-state underground Jewish defence force which became the nucleus of the Israel Defence Force (Israeli army).

Hashomer Hatzair: Zionist-socialist pioneering youth movement founded in 1916 whose aim was to educate Jewish youth for kibbutz life in Palestine.

Irgun: Underground Jewish military organization formed in 1931 as an alternative to the more "defensive" Haganah. Carried out reprisals against Arabs of which the massacre at Deir Yassin is the most notorious.

Kahane, Meir (Rabbi): American born Rabbi and Knesset member who advocates the voluntary resettlement or forced eviction of all Arabs in Israel and the West Bank to Jordan or elsewhere.

Kibbutz: Israel's communal agricultural settlements where all property is held in common.

Kipa: Skull cap worn by religiously observant Jews.

Knesset: Israel's 120 member unicameral parliament.

Kosher: "Fit" or "proper": usually refers to foods allowed or disallowed under Jewish religious law.

Labour Zionists: A movement founded in Russia at the end of the nineteenth century based on a Jewish proletariat whose ideology was a combination of Zionism and socialism.

Law of the Return: Guarantees citizenship to any Jew wishing to immigrate to Israel, providing he/she is no danger to public health or security.

Levinger, Moshe (Rabbi): Leader of the Gush Emunim movement.

Likud: "Unity": coalition of right-wing political parties that came to power in 1977. Advocates retention of all territories captured in 1967 war.

Mapai: Israel Labour Party founded in 1930.

Mapam: United Workers Party founded in 1948. Ideologically left-wing with ties to international socialism. Supports class struggle, separation of state and religion, freedom of conscience and worship and complete equality for Arab minority.

Metanoia: Greek word meaning "to change one's mind". In Christian theology it connotes repentance.

Moshav: Israeli agricultural settlement where land and machinery are individually owned in contrast to the kibbutz where there is no private property.

Muezzim: Islamic official who calls the faithful to prayer five times daily and to public worship on Fridays.

Muslim feast: Celebration marking the end of Ramadan — the month of fasting.

National Religious Party: Political party advocating legislation based on the laws of the Torah and Jewish tradition.

Neve Shalom: Village near Jerusalem inhabited by Arabs and Jews as a sign of the possibility of peaceful co-existence.

Palmach: Strike force of the Haganah established in 1941. Later became part of the Israel Defence Force.

Peace Now: Largest and most well known of Israeli peace movements. Founded in 1978 by reserve military officers as a protest against the Begin government's hesitancy to move on a peace agenda.

Peres, Shimon: Israeli prime minister 1984-86; currently foreign minister.

Phalange: The Maronite Christian Lebanese militia.

Pogrom: "Spontaneous" civilian riots against Jews in Russia (1881-1921). The accompanying looting, murder and rape caused massive Jewish emigration.

Sabra and Chatila: The September 1982 massacre of hundreds of Palestinians in the two Beirut refugee camps. While the massacre was carried out by Phalangists, Israel bore indirect responsibility because it was with the agreement of the Israeli military that the Phalangists were allowed into the camps.

Seder: Ceremony observed in Jewish homes on the first night of Passover.

Sephardi: That part of the Jewish community which traces its ancestry to Spain and Portugal.

Shamir, Yitzak: Israel's current prime minister.

Sharon, Ariel (Gen.): Israeli general and politician associated with the right-wing Herut Party. Praised for his military ability and criticized for his ruthlessness. Chief planner of the 1982 Lebanon invasion.

Torah: "Teaching" or "doctrine": consists of the Pentateuch and the entire body of traditional Jewish teaching and literature.

Tri-partite Aggression: The joint Israeli, French and British attack on the Suez Canal Zone in 1956.

Two-State Solution: Solving the Israeli/Palestinian conflict and providing self-determination for Palestinians by the creation of a Palestinian state in the West Bank and Gaza which would live side by side and at peace with Israel.

United Arab Republic: The 1958-61 national union of Egypt and Syria.

Village leagues: Groups of West Bank Arabs appointed by Israeli authorities to fulfill local aspirations for self-government. League members were perceived as quislings and were repudiated by the Palestinian community.

Western Wall: Most hallowed spot in Jewish religious and national consciousness. Section of the western supporting wall of the Temple Mount which has remained intact since the Second Temple's destruction in 70 C.E.

Yad Vashem: Jerusalem memorial to the victims of the Holocaust. Name taken from Isaiah 56:5 "I will give, in my house and within my walls, a monument and a name better than sons and daughters; I will give them an everlasting name that shall never be effaced."

Yeshiva: Jewish traditional academy dedicated to study of the Talmud.

Many of these definitions were taken from the *Encyclopedia Britannica* and the *Encyclopedia Judaica*